剑桥双语分级阅读·小说馆（第2版）

原版系列编辑 Philip Prowse



# Staying Together

# 相守

[英] 朱迪斯·威尔逊 著

杨絮名 编译

北京语言大学出版社
BEIJING LANGUAGE AND CULTURE UNIVERSITY PRESS

CAMBRIDGE UNIVERSITY PRESS

社图号25021



北京市版权局著作权合同登记图字：01-2024-3256号

**图书在版编目（CIP）数据**

相守 ： 英汉对照 / （英）朱迪斯·威尔逊（Judith Wilson）著 ； 杨絮名编译. -- 2版. -- 北京 ： 北京语言大学出版社, 2025. 3. -- （剑桥双语分级阅读小说馆）. -- ISBN 978-7-5619-6740-9

Ⅰ. H319.4

中国国家版本馆CIP数据核字第20252XM891号

**相守**
XIANGSHOU

---

**责任编辑：**于华颖
**责任印制：**周 燚

---

**出版发行：**北京语言大学出版社
**社　　址：**北京市海淀区学院路 15 号，100083
**网　　址：**www.blcup.com
**电子信箱：**service@blcup.com
**电　　话：**编 辑 部 010-8230 1019
发 行 部 010-8230 3650/3591/3648
北语书店 010-8230 3653
网购咨询 010-8230 3908
**印　　刷：**东港股份有限公司

---

**版　　次：**2017 年 6 月第 1 版　2025 年 3 月第 2 版　**印　　次：**2025 年 3 月第 1 次印刷
**开　　本：**880 毫米 × 1230 毫米　1/32　**印　　张：**6.25
**字　　数：**148 千字　**定　　价：**23.00 元

---

PRINTED IN CHINA
凡有印装质量问题，本社负责调换。售后QQ号1367565611，电话010-82303590

# Preface

# 前言

“剑桥双语分级阅读·小说馆”是一套从剑桥大学出版社引进的面向非英语国家英语学习者的分级系列读物，由英语语言教学专家及小说作家合力创作。创作过程历时三十余年，出版后受到世界各地英语教师和英语学习者的喜爱，许多读本再版多次，三十余年来畅销不衰，成为受全球英语学习者青睐的优秀读本。

本系列读物具有以下突出特色：

1. 是原创英语读物，而非改编自普通作品的读物。因此，阅读本系列读物，我们读到的是原汁原味的原创英语，而非人为改编过的二手英语。

2. 是当代优秀短篇小说，而非年代久远的小说。因此，阅读本系列读物，我们读到的是当今鲜活的、学了就能用的英语，而非穿越时空的、学了用不上的英语；了解的是与读者同时代不同国家人们的生活和思想，而非隔代人的生活、文化和风土人情。

3. 是专为非英语国家的英语学习者量身定制的读物，而非为英语母语者所写的大众读物。因此，本系列读物是中国读者首选的英语学习读物。

4. 是英美知名小说家和英语语言教学专家合力创作的读物。小说家保障了读物的可读性与可欣赏性，英语语言教学专家保障了读物语言作为英语习得材料的科学性与可学性。本系列读物中的多个读本都曾在世界上颇具影响力的“语言学习者文学奖”（Language Learner Literature Award）评选中获得大奖。因此，阅读本系列读物，我们会在欣赏小说的同时，自然而然地、有效地提高自己的英语水平。

5. 本系列读物的故事题材丰富多样，包括侦探、情感、历险、悬疑、人文、科幻、喜剧等，读者可以随心选择自己喜欢的类别阅读；故事内容生动有趣，故事情节引人入胜、扣人心弦，读者一旦开始阅读，就想一口气读完，使阅读真正升华到“悦读”。

6. 随书附赠的音频材料内容精彩，是专业配音员的演绎再创作。听着它，我们犹如在听广播剧、听评书，又仿佛是在听电影、听话剧……这种聆听英语的享受将彻底扫除学生对英语听力的畏难心理。

7. 本系列读物所使用的语言，既有英式英语，也有美式英语，对应的音频材料也相应分为英音和美音，读者可根据自己的喜好来选择。

8. 本系列近百本读物根据《欧洲语言共同参考框架》(CEFR)和剑桥大学外语考评部开发的ESOL考试的标准来确定级别划分，是建立在科学研究和实践基础之上的分级。全套共分七个级别（与中国学生英语基础水平的大致对应关系，请参见图书封底表格），读者可根据自己的英语基础选择相应级别的读本来学习。

为了更好地帮助中国学生学习和欣赏，“剑桥双语分级阅读·小说馆”从剑桥大学出版社原版引进后又增加了以下内容：

1. 增加了适量的辅助学习内容，包括“读前思考”“读后活动”“学习指导”三个板块，其中“学习指导”板块又包括生词、短语和表达、文化点滴、阅读练习四项内容。增加这些板块的目的是全方位帮助学生提升英语阅读能力，扩充词汇量，扫除阅读中的文化障碍，增强对英语小说的鉴赏能力。

2. 增加了小说全文的参考译文。出于语言学习的考虑，译文多采用直译，但也尽量符合中文的表达习惯。

值得一提的是，所增加的辅助学习内容和参考译文，全部由来自全国不同省市知名中学（包括人大附中、北大附中、清华附中、黄冈中学、上海中学等三十余所中学）的一线英语教师完成。这些一线教师的加盟，确保了所加内容与中国学生的英语学习特点和学习需求相吻合，为学生阅读和欣赏读物、提高英语水平给予恰到好处的助力。

英语阅读是英语课堂的延伸和补充，也是培养英语语感、提高英语水平的有效途径。选择一套好的英语读物，收获的将不仅仅是语言的进步。欢迎年轻朋友们来到“剑桥双语分级阅读·小说馆”，打开一本本好书，品味一个个好故事，为实现梦想搭建桥梁。

北京语言大学出版社

# Contents 目录

## People in the story

## 故事中的人物

**Ikuko Kanazawa:** an office worker in Tokyo

金泽郁子：一名东京的办公室职员

**Hiroshi Masuda:** Ikuko's boyfriend

增田宏：郁子的男朋友

**Bernard Chiluba:** an African student

伯纳德·奇卢巴：一名非洲学生

**Lucretia:** a Brazilian student

柳克丽霞：一名巴西学生

**Mike:** a photography teacher

迈克：一位摄影教师

**Joyce Mutanga:** a media-scientist

乔伊斯·缪坦加：一位传媒学者

**Fatima:** head of the Red Sea Research Centre

法蒂玛：红海研究中心主任

**Taka:** a researcher at the Centre

阿贵：中心的一位研究员

**Sven:** a researcher at the Centre

斯文：中心的一位研究员

# Before reading

## 读前思考

1. Read the back cover, contents and people in the story. What sort of story is this?

2. If you have the recording, listen to Chapter 1.

# PART 1
# GOING AWAY

# Chapter 1
# The promise

'Are we really eating here, Hiroshi?' Ikuko stopped by the door of the expensive Tokyo restaurant, looking unsure.

Hiroshi smiled as he held the door open for her. 'Of course. It's your birthday. Everything's arranged.'

Inside, the big room was almost full. Well-dressed people talked softly together. The waiter showed Ikuko and Hiroshi to their table and brought them a bottle of wine. Ikuko felt a little nervous. This wasn't the sort of place they usually came to. But when Hiroshi smiled at her across the table, with his dark hair falling into his eyes as usual, she felt better.

Hiroshi raised his glass. 'Happy birthday, Ikuko,' he said. 'How does it feel to be twenty-three?'

She smiled. 'I can't believe it. I still feel sixteen.'

As they came to the end of their meal, they fell silent and looked at one another. There was a candle burning on the table and Ikuko could see its light in Hiroshi's eyes. After a moment Hiroshi put his hand in the pocket of his jacket, and brought out a little box.

'Ikuko,' he said, and then stopped. 'Ikuko, you know how I feel about you. I've never met anyone else like you. I'd like you to have this. I'd like us to stay together always.'

He handed the box across the table to Ikuko. She opened it, her hands shaking. Inside there was a ring. It was a simple ring, perfectly chosen for her by someone who loved her. But part of her was thinking, 'This isn't happening to me.' It was as if she was watching someone in a movie.

She knew her parents liked Hiroshi. He was a considerate man who had done well in his company and would look after Ikuko, their only daughter. Her friends liked him too – he was kind and always ready to help anyone with a problem. Ikuko knew that she liked being with Hiroshi and that he'd never made her feel unhappy for a moment. She couldn't imagine her life without him. So why did the idea of marrying him seem like a door closing on the future?

Hiroshi put his hand on hers. Ikuko looked up at him. 'Hiroshi, I do love you. But...if we get married now, what will I do then?'

'I'll look after you. You won't need to work any

more. You'll have time to do all the things you want to do.' Hiroshi spoke with his usual optimism. 'You can carry on with your English classes and do more of the things you enjoy...things like your photography. We can get a flat – maybe even a house one day, with a garden for the children.'

'It sounds lovely,' replied Ikuko. 'But I'm younger than you. I've never really done anything. I just went straight into the Hayakawa company after college. You've done lots of things – you've travelled and studied in America. You've learnt something about the world.'

'Ikuko, people talk about travelling as such a great thing, but what I found is that I like Japan best. I had American friends, sure, but we never got very close. You can never really understand someone from another culture. Believe me, the most beautiful places and the people who matter most are the ones in your own country, your own home.'

Ikuko thought she'd be happy with Hiroshi. She'd imagined spending her life with him – just not so soon. She knew she would have to tell him how she felt. But before she could find the words, Hiroshi found them for her.

'Ikuko, I remember how much I once wanted to travel. And I don't want you to miss that chance if it's what you really want. So if you want to go and study for a few months, in America or in England, I can wait for you.'

'He understands so well,' thought Ikuko. Suddenly, everything seemed clear.

'Yes,' she said at last. 'I think I need a few months to see things for myself. To grow up a little more. Will you wait for me? Then I'll come back and we can get married.'

'Don't grow up too much, Ikuko. I like you just as you are,' said Hiroshi. Gently he put the ring onto her finger.

* * *

Two months later, Ikuko turned off her computer in the big office in the Hayakawa building for the last time. Outside, the Tokyo sky was dark and lights were already shining in the tall office buildings. She got up from her desk and went across the room, past the desk of old Mr Honma, the office manager. He looked up as she walked past. 'Well, Ikuko, so it's goodbye. We'll miss you. Where are you going to in England, anyway? London?'

'No – a place called Birmingham,' Ikuko replied.

'Never heard of it. Is it beautiful there?' he asked.

'I don't know. But I'll bring lots of photos back.'

She went to get her jacket. It was a cold December day and she pulled on a warm hat in front of the mirror. She looked at herself. The girl looking back at her out of the mirror did not look very different from the girl who had started work there more than two years before: a pale serious face with long straight hair and a pointed chin. She wondered how this next year would change her – living in England, and then the wedding.

On the train journey home, Ikuko sat and thought about the past two years. She'd been lucky to get the job in the Hayakawa company. Lucky because it was a good company and she found the work interesting. And lucky because she'd met Hiroshi there.

She remembered the day they'd met. It had been late on a Friday afternoon. She'd only been working there for a few weeks and she was still feeling unsure of herself. She was entering numbers on the computer for a sales program. But the results looked wrong. She took a deep breath and went up to Mr Honma's desk to tell him. Mr Honma hadn't been very helpful, but he'd arranged for one of the programmers to have a look.

Half an hour later Ikuko had looked up to see a tall man, young and with rather untidy hair, coming across the room towards her. He stopped and introduced himself.

'I'm Hiroshi Masuda. I hear you have some problems with the sales program,' he said.

Ikuko explained and Hiroshi listened carefully, then sat down and did some work on the computer. Suddenly he stopped and looked up at her, brushing his hair out of his eyes. He was excited. 'You're absolutely right. There's a mistake in the program. I knew there was something wrong with the numbers we were getting. Now we can change it. Thanks!' He stood up. 'Anyway, it's probably time you got off home. Do you live far away?'

'In Ome. It's an hour away on the train,' said Ikuko.

'Oh, yes, I know. In fact I go through Ome on my way home. So we've been travelling on the same train. I'm surprised we haven't seen one another before.'

'Well, the trains are so crowded,' Ikuko said.

'Yes,' he said, 'but I'd notice you, even in a crowd.'

And that was how it had begun. Sitting in the train now, two years later, Ikuko remembered the early days of their friendship: meals in small restaurants, walks in the park – slowly getting to know each other. They discovered that they'd both gone to the same Junior High school, although Hiroshi had been four years ahead of Ikuko. After leaving university, he'd gone to do a computing course in America. He'd done very well, but hadn't enjoyed life in America and decided instead to return to Tokyo.

In those first days of new love, Ikuko and Hiroshi had spent almost all their free time together. Ikuko liked his gentleness and understanding. It was the perfect relationship. No arguments or bad surprises. Wasn't that what she wanted?

'Ome...Ome.' Ikuko heard the name of her station and woke suddenly from her thoughts. She got off and walked out of the crowded station. On her way home, she stopped at a department store – she still had to buy a suitcase for her trip. As she walked to the suitcase department, she passed a shelf of diaries. She stopped. That wasn't what she'd come for. She looked at the diaries a moment longer and then chose one with a plain white cover.

In the suitcase department, she quickly found what she was looking for.

'I'll take that one,' she said, pointing to a blue suitcase. It was expensive, but she was going a long way. And she could use it for her honeymoon later on.

* * *

A few days later Ikuko was sitting in Narita International Airport with Hiroshi. The blue suitcase had already been checked in on the London flight, and they were having one last coffee together.

The two of them had hardly spoken on the way to the airport. Ikuko wondered if she was making a terrible mistake. 'It's only for six months,' she said to Hiroshi, trying to persuade herself as much as him.

'A lot can happen in six months,' he said. 'I don't want to lose you. Remember you promised to come back.'

Ikuko looked at her ring. 'I'll come back,' she said.

They said goodbye, but as she went through to the departure lounge she looked back one last time. Hiroshi was still standing there, his hair falling into his eyes, looking lost and lonely in the middle of the airport crowds.

# Chapter 2
# The blue suitcase

'Can you describe the suitcase?' asked the woman at the desk in Heathrow Airport. Ikuko felt like crying. It had been a bad flight. She'd been sitting next to two children who were noisy and who couldn't sit still. Ikuko hadn't been able to sleep at all. And now her suitcase was lost. With her clothes, her camera – everything.

She said slowly in English, 'It was blue...'

The woman smiled at her kindly. 'Don't worry. Just fill in this form. I'm sure we'll find it. It will probably be on the next plane. We'll send it on.'

Slowly Ikuko wrote a description of the suitcase and what was in it, and the address she would be staying at: Selly Park Hostel, Oak Road, Selly Oak, Birmingham.

Four long hours later the taxi drove up in front of a big old house with trees around it. It was seven o'clock. It had been a long, difficult journey from Heathrow Airport – the London underground, the train to Birmingham and the taxi from the station to the hostel.

Ikuko walked up to the hostel. She thought the building looked like pictures of churches she'd seen with its dark stone walls and pointed windows. Two students came out of the door, talking in a language Ikuko didn't understand. She went inside. There was no-one at the reception desk, but there was a sign: 'Ring bell for service'. She rang it.

After a moment a door opened and a woman came out. 'Can I help you?'

'I'm Ikuko...Ikuko Kanazawa.'

'Oh, yes. We were expecting you. You're in room 31. Come along, I'll show you. Where's your suitcase?'

Ikuko started to tell her, but the woman didn't seem to be listening.

'Oh dear. Never mind,' she said. 'Now, here's your room. Dinner's finished now, but there are plenty of restaurants five minutes away on Bristol Road if you want something to eat. Breakfast's at eight – back in the main building, on the ground floor. OK? Do you understand?'

'Yes,' Ikuko said as the door closed, leaving her alone. But she wasn't sure she had understood. The woman sounded different from the recordings she'd listened to in her English lessons. Maybe it was because Ikuko was so tired.

She looked around the room: a bed, a desk, a lamp. She wanted a bath, but she had no towel. She wasn't hungry, and anyway she couldn't face going out into the cold strange streets that night. She wanted to ring Hiroshi – but in Japan it would be four o'clock in the morning.

The room felt cold and she got into bed to try to keep warm. She was tired but her mind was still active. She took her new diary out of her handbag and started to write in English.

*9 January 2000*
*Today I arrived in England. It's very exciting.*

She thought for a moment. 'Who am I writing this for?' she wondered. 'Will I show it to Hiroshi? Or is it just for me? Anyway, I should write the truth.' She started again.

*Today I arrived in England. My suitcase is lost. The journey was quite difficult. I'm disappointed that I can't understand English people better. Now I'm in my room in the student hostel. I feel so lonely. I miss Hiroshi. Maybe he was right about travelling.*

She put down her pen feeling close to tears. This was not how she had expected to feel on her first day in England. She put her head down on her pillow – maybe if she had a rest she'd feel better...

* * *

There was a knock on the door and a man's voice. 'Ikuko Kanazawa?'

The room was dark and for a minute Ikuko didn't know where she was. She turned on the light and looked at her watch. It was seven o'clock on Monday morning and she was in England.

There was another knock, and then footsteps going away. Ikuko got out of bed and realised she was still wearing all her clothes. She felt hot and uncomfortable.

She went to the door and opened it. A man was disappearing down the corridor. She could only see his back – black hair and a red jacket. And in front of the door was her blue suitcase.

# Chapter 3
# The first week

Ikuko carried the suitcase into her room, feeling much better. Now she could have a shower and change her clothes. But first she must ring Hiroshi. She got her mobile phone out of her handbag and dialled his number.

'So what's Birmingham like?' he asked, sounding very far away. He'd never understood why she'd wanted to study in Birmingham and not somewhere more famous like Oxford or Cambridge. But she hadn't wanted to stay in a tourist centre, even if it was beautiful. She'd wanted to see how English people really lived.

But now she wasn't so sure. She walked over to the window of her small bedroom and looked out. There was a narrow road with cars parked along it, and a few trees with no leaves left on them. Everything looked cold and dark in the early morning light.

'Well,' she said, 'it's sort of grey.'

An hour later, Ikuko found the dining room of the hostel. She walked in shyly. There was a smell of fried food and a sound of quiet talking. She looked around and saw that, although there were some people in groups, quite a few people were sitting alone. 'Maybe I'm not the only person who's just arrived,' she thought.

A large woman came over and said, 'Are you new here, dear? Do you want a cooked breakfast?'

Ikuko looked confused. What was a cooked breakfast? But the woman became impatient. 'Bacon and eggs?' she said loudly.

'Yes...yes, please,' Ikuko replied.

As she sat alone eating, Ikuko wondered if any of the students in the room were English. She could see a group of Japanese students – a boy with bright yellow hair and earrings, and two girls dressed in tight fashionable clothes. Nearer to her was a group of girls talking in English and another language. Everyone looked very young.

'Will I have anything in common with these people?' she thought. 'Maybe I should just get a flight back to Japan.'

She took a deep breath. She'd got her suitcase. Things weren't so bad. Time to go to her English class. She finished her breakfast and walked out of the room.

Ten minutes later she walked out into the street. She took out the map she'd been given with directions to the language centre and started to walk. She was supposed to get a bus, but where was the bus stop? She tried to work it out from her map.

Then someone spoke to her in Japanese. 'Are you going to the language centre?'

She turned round. It was the Japanese boy with yellow hair. He was with two other students, a dark-haired girl and a taller boy.

'Yes...yes,' she said to the Japanese boy. 'On the 65 bus?'

'That's right.' Then he continued in English, 'Come with us. We're all going, too.'

And sitting in the pub that evening with a glass of warm beer in front of her which took her all evening to finish, Ikuko realised she already had friends. Sitting opposite her was the Japanese boy with yellow hair. His name was Toshi. 'Everyone calls me crazy Toshi,' he said, laughing. He'd been in England for a long time and seemed to know everyone. Next to him was Pietro from Italy. And sitting next to Ikuko was Lucretia, the dark-haired girl who had been with Toshi that morning. She was from South America.

From a town called Recife, in Brazil. Lucretia had shown her where it was on the map in the classroom.

Ikuko liked Lucretia's warm smile, her green eyes and her confident English. She talked so quickly that Ikuko could hardly follow.

'Oh, yes,' said Lucretia, as they sat talking in the pub. 'But my writing! No good at all! I have to improve.'

'How long have you been here?' asked Ikuko.

'Three months. I need to pass my IELTS exam, then I can do Business Studies at the University.'

Later, they all walked back to the hostel together through the dark streets.

'Who wants some good Italian coffee?' asked Pietro. But suddenly all Ikuko wanted was to be on her own. She said good night to them and went to her room. But before she went to sleep she got out her diary.

*10 January 2000*

*What a long day...so many things happened. My suitcase arrived. I went to my first English class and made some friends from different countries. It's very hard speaking in English all day. Everyone's friendly, but they're all a bit younger than me. I like Lucretia. She's very lively, and kind, too. We went to the pub.*

*It was hard to understand people, it was so noisy. Everyone seemed to be having a good time, though. But it's not quite what I expected. What did I expect, really? I don't know.*

* * *

As she sat in the coffee bar waiting for Lucretia on Friday afternoon, Ikuko couldn't believe that she'd only been in England for five days. It seemed much longer. She already felt at home in the hostel and was getting to know the tree-lined streets of her little corner of Birmingham.

She wandered over to the notice board on the wall of the coffee bar. Among the notices for discos and films there was one which caught her attention.

**Photography club.**
**Next meeting: Saturday 15 January at 2 pm.**
**Room 261.**
**Pictures of people – Bernard Chiluba**
**All welcome.**

She thought of her camera lying unused on the desk in her room. She used to belong to a photography club in Junior High school. It would be nice to learn a little bit more about photography – and to take some pictures to show Hiroshi. Saturday afternoon. That was tomorrow. She wrote down the place and time.

Just then Lucretia came up behind her. 'Oh, photography. That's supposed to be a good club. But Saturdays are for shopping. Don't you want to go into town instead?'

'Thanks, but I don't like shopping much,' replied Ikuko.

'No?' said Lucretia, looking surprised. 'Funny, I love shopping. OK, well, call round to my room about five o'clock. I'll show you what I've bought.'

* * *

At two o'clock the next day Ikuko shyly opened the door of room 261. It was a small room full of people talking to one another. She didn't know anyone there, but a young man with curly brown hair and glasses came over to her.

'Hi. Welcome. Have you come to join the club?'

'Yes...I think so,' said Ikuko.

'Great. I'm Mike. I'm the one who started the club. And you're...?'

'Ikuko. What do you do in the club?'

'Well, it's really just a chance to get together and help one another,' Mike explained. 'We've got a darkroom, so you can develop your pictures here if you want...'

'Develop?' Ikuko didn't understand.

'Yes, instead of taking the film to a photoshop, you can learn to do it yourself – just black and white though, not colour. And we go out together, taking pictures. Usually just in Birmingham, but sometimes we go to the country.'

He spoke quickly, but Ikuko managed to understand. She was pleased. Except for her teachers, she hadn't really spoken to many English people.

'Have you done much photography in...Japan, is it?' asked Mike.

'Just a little. But I'd like to learn a bit more,' Ikuko replied.

'Well, today Bernard's going to show us some of the pictures he's taken of people in Birmingham. Bernard Chiluba, over there.' Mike pointed at a tall man standing with his back to them – black hair, very short and curly, and a red jacket. Where had she seen that jacket before?

Hearing his name, the man turned round and came up to them. His skin was very dark brown, almost black, smooth and shining. He seemed a little older than the other students.

'Bernard, this is Ikuko,' said Mike.

Bernard smiled, a wide smile, his teeth very white in his dark face. Ikuko noticed that his smile was crooked, a little wider on one side than the other. He held out his hand and she shook it, still looking at him.

'Hello, Ikuko.'

His hand held hers powerfully. His voice was deep and she liked the soft slow way he said her name. He continued talking: 'But I think we're neighbours. Are you Ikuko with the blue suitcase?'

And then Ikuko remembered the red jacket she'd seen disappearing down the corridor on the first morning.

She let go of his hand, feeling suddenly shy. 'Oh... thank you...yes, it was my suitcase. How...how did you know it was mine?'

'I was just leaving the hostel when it arrived from the airport. It was early in the morning. The receptionist was busy – so I said I'd take it up for her.'

'Oh, thank you...that was very kind.' She noticed how clearly he spoke. Not too fast like all the other people she'd met, not hurrying on before she had time to reply.

'So you're from Japan?' he asked.

'Yes...and you?'

'I'm from Zambia. In Africa.'

Around them people were starting to sit down. 'Right, excuse us, Ikuko,' said Mike, and he went up to the front and introduced Bernard's talk. Ikuko listened to Bernard's deep voice explaining the pictures. She had never seen any like them before. He had taken them all in Birmingham, but the people in them seemed to come from every corner of the world: Jamaica, Pakistan, China. Ikuko wondered if she could ever learn to make silent faces come alive like that.

At the end of the meeting she went up to Bernard. 'Thank you. They're wonderful pictures.'

Bernard smiled at her. 'Thanks. It's something I really enjoy doing.' He looked at her a little uncertainly. 'We're just going for coffee. Would you like to come?'

Ikuko looked at her watch. It was half past four. She remembered that she was meeting Lucretia back at the hostel. 'No...I'm sorry, I can't. I have to meet someone.'

'Oh, OK,' he said and turned away.

# Chapter 4
# City centre

The next Saturday Ikuko woke up early. She looked out of her window and saw the sun for almost the first time, shining on the trees in the garden next door. What a beautiful morning! 'A whole day free,' she thought. 'I really should be a bit braver. I've not really seen anything of Birmingham yet.' She decided to go and explore.

An hour later she was waiting for the bus. When it arrived she asked for a ticket to the town centre and sat down in an empty seat near the front. The doors closed, but there was the sound of running steps and the doors opened again to let one more person on. Ikuko saw a red jacket and recognised the deep voice speaking to the driver. 'Thank you. City centre, please.'

He had almost walked past Ikuko when she suddenly heard herself say, 'Bernard?'

He looked up, surprised. 'Oh, Ikuko. I didn't see you,' he said as he sat down next to her. She could feel him very close in the narrow bus seat. They were quiet for a moment, then they both started talking at the same time.

'Are you...'

'I haven't seen you...'

They laughed. 'Go on,' said Bernard.

'I haven't seen you...are you still staying in the hostel?'

'Sure. But I get up earlier than most people. I'm usually the first person at breakfast.'

'You're not studying at the language centre, are you?'

'No, I'm in the Department of Education. I'm doing a teaching diploma. So I'm over at the university most of the day – and I eat at the university in the evenings, too.'

'Is your course difficult?' she asked him.

'Yes, there's a lot of work. But I'm used to hard work. At home I'm a teacher already. But I got a scholarship from the government to pay to come here and do the diploma.'

She wondered what his life was like, back in Zambia. 'Do you live in the capital?' she asked.

'No. I come from the north of Zambia, a small town called Mungwi. There's just a school and a few shops. We don't even have a hospital. No big buildings at all.

Not like Birmingham.' He smiled, the crooked smile she'd noticed before. 'And what are you going to do in Birmingham this morning? Are you going shopping?'

'No,' Ikuko replied. 'I just wanted to have a look at Birmingham.'

'It's a fine city. I like it,' he said. 'Lots of people complain about it. But it's alive. It's always growing, always changing.'

Around them now were tall buildings shining in the sun. Then the bus went down a narrow street and stopped.

'This is where we get off.' They followed the other passengers off the bus. Then Bernard turned to her. 'If you want...I could show you a bit of Birmingham.'

'Yes, please,' said Ikuko. 'I'd like that a lot.'

They walked together through the centre of Birmingham, in the middle of the Saturday crowds. Bernard showed her the little cathedral in its tiny green garden, the art gallery, and the new shops and restaurants built where the old factories had once stood. They talked about what they saw, about Birmingham and their own countries. Ikuko hardly noticed her tired feet or the cold wind.

Then Bernard looked at his watch. 'It's lunchtime.

It's after one o'clock. What do you want to do?'

'Shall we go to a restaurant?' she suggested. 'Or we could go back to the hostel?'

'I can't face hostel food,' said Bernard. 'Let's go to an Indian restaurant. I know a good one near here.'

The restaurant was small, but warm and friendly. The Indian waiter was pleased to see them. 'Hi, Bernard. You all right, then? Where's your camera?'

'You've seen him before,' said Bernard to Ikuko. 'In one of the photos.' He showed her how to eat the spicy meat with pieces of bread in her fingers. 'This is how we eat at home; we don't use knives and forks. The food tastes better like this. But in Zambia we mostly eat *nshima* instead of bread or potatoes. Oh, I miss *nshima*!'

'Yes, I miss rice. They have rice in the hostel but it's different from the rice in Japan. It's hard,' said Ikuko.

'And in Japan you eat with those sticks, don't you?'

'Chopsticks? Yes, it's easy. I'll show you! But we don't use them all the time – sometimes we eat the western way.'

'Do you live with your family?' he asked. It was the first personal question he'd asked her.

'Yes.' She wondered if she should tell him about

Hiroshi. But it didn't seem the right moment. Bernard was quiet for a moment, too. She wondered if he was thinking of his home. 'How about you?' she asked. 'Do you live with your parents?'

'No, my parents are very old. They live alone...' He looked as if he was going to say something more but then was silent again.

Ikuko felt this was not something he wanted to talk about. She waited a minute then changed the subject. 'How long have you been taking photos?'

'Oh, a long time. It's always been my hobby. But I'm starting a photography business of my own,' he said.

'As well as teaching?' Ikuko asked.

'Yes. It'll be hard work, but I can do it. People always want photographs. They need them for their passports and other papers, and they want them for special times too – weddings and other ceremonies. There's no photographer in Mungwi, so if I can develop my own pictures it will mean I can earn more money. How about you, Ikuko? Do you have a job in Japan?'

'No, not any more,' she answered. 'I left my job.'

'So what will you do when you go back to Japan?'

Ikuko looked at the ring on her finger. 'I don't know exactly,' she said. 'There's someone...'

'I see,' said Bernard. 'I understand.'

*22 January 2000*

*Today I spent the morning in Birmingham with Bernard. He showed me so many things. And tonight he's invited me to meet his friends. We're going to listen to Zambian music and eat Zambian food. I hope we can be good friends. He's different from anyone else I've met here. Different from anyone I've ever met.*

# Chapter 5
# Snowfall

'So you're off with Bernard again this weekend?' It was Saturday morning and Lucretia was sitting in Ikuko's room, drinking coffee. She looked at Ikuko over the top of her coffee cup.

'It's just the photography club. We're going to the country. To a place called Broadway,' Ikuko replied.

Lucretia raised her eyebrows, but didn't say anything. Ikuko knew what she was thinking.

'We're just friends, Lucretia. Really. He knows there's someone in Japan.'

'But, Ikuko, does that someone in Japan know about Bernard?' Lucretia asked.

'It's not like that,' Ikuko began. 'Bernard and I...In some ways we're very close. We like the same things. But we don't talk about him and me and things like that.' She looked at her ring. 'I haven't said anything to Hiroshi. I don't want to worry him...about nothing.'

'But is it nothing?' asked Lucretia. 'Because sometimes when I see you two together, it seems as if there's more.'

'No, there's no more. We go for walks. We talk a lot. I'm finding out about so many different places and people...about Africa, about Zambia: the stories, the music. I'm learning how to dance.' Ikuko remembered the feel of Bernard's hand in hers as they danced together.

When Ikuko was with Bernard, everything seemed fine. So why did she feel so confused?

'Be careful, Ikuko.'

'I'll be all right, Lucretia. Really.'

*　　*　　*

'OK everyone, let's go!' Mike started up the minibus and they drove off through the grey streets, then along the motorway and into the countryside. Ikuko and Bernard looked out of the window at the frozen fields and cloudy sky. Ikuko realised that she was turning her ring round and round on her finger. Bernard was unusually quiet, too. They turned off the motorway and slowed down as the road got narrower and the hills got steeper. Soon they came into a village and the minibus stopped by the side of the street.

'Right, everyone, we're here,' said Mike as he came round and opened the side door. 'I hope you've all got warm clothes on – it's freezing! I suggest we have a look round the village and take any pictures before the light goes. Then meet back at the tea-rooms here at four o'clock.'

The cold wind hit them as they got off the bus. They were in the middle of a street with small old houses on both sides. Although it was only two o'clock, the houses all had lights on. They walked along together, heads down against the cold. Some of the group stopped and went into the little shops, but Mike, Ikuko and Bernard carried on until they reached an old church. They walked down the path to the church door. On either side of the path, there were grey tombstones with the names of people who had died and been laid there under the ground hundreds of years ago. There were small white flowers among the tombstones.

'What are they called?' asked Ikuko.

'They're snowdrops – the first spring flowers,' said Mike.

Ikuko bent down with her camera, trying to take a picture of the small flowers, but it was already too dark. A few flakes of snow started to fall.

'Snow,' said Bernard. 'So this is what it looks like. I've never seen it before.' He turned to Ikuko, smiling.

'Let's go inside the church,' said Mike.

Inside it smelt of stone and candles. They walked around quietly.

'Ikuko, look.' Bernard showed her an old tombstone. There was a stone woman on it, lying with her hands crossed. Ikuko looked at it, wondering about the woman's life. She looked young – about the same age as Ikuko. Suddenly, a flash lit the darkness and Ikuko looked up in surprise. Bernard stood there with his camera. 'You looked lovely standing there, as if you were made of stone yourself,' he said.

When they came out of the church it was snowing harder and the ground was already white.

'Let's try to get some pictures of it,' said Bernard.

But Mike was worried. 'I don't like this,' he said. 'We'd better get back.' They hurried back to the tea-room and found the others there already. Ikuko wanted to stay and get warm but there was no time.

'Sorry,' said Mike. 'But it's a bad road until we get to the motorway. We need to leave as soon as possible.'

They got back into the minibus. Ikuko and Bernard were sitting near the front with Bernard next to the window. Mike got into the driver's seat and set off, driving slowly and carefully. Everyone was quiet. The minibus started to go up a hill, very slowly.

Suddenly there were lights in front of them, then a bang that seemed to go right through Ikuko. She heard screams and felt herself being thrown towards the front window. There was a sound of breaking glass.

A second later Ikuko was lying across the minibus seat, almost on the floor. Bernard had his arms tightly round her.

'Bernard...?'

'Yes...are you OK?'

'I think so.' She pulled herself up carefully. At the back of the bus people were shouting. But at the front everything was quiet. She got up and moved towards the driver's seat. The engine was still running but Mike was not moving. He lay face down in his seat, his hair covered in broken glass, the wet snow blowing in through the broken window.

Ikuko stretched over and turned off the engine. She could hear voices now outside. The driver of the other vehicle – a van – had got out and was talking to the other students. She could just see them, dark against the snow.

She bent over Mike and gently lifted up his face, frightened of what she might find. Bernard came up behind her and she turned to him. 'He's breathing,' she said. 'We need to get help for him. My mobile phone... It's in my bag – probably on the floor somewhere. Can you get it?'

A minute later, Bernard came back with the phone. But she realised she didn't know what number to ring, who to ask for or what to say. She gave it to Bernard. The people outside kept on talking. Suddenly there seemed to be nothing to do except wait, as the snow continued to fall.

Much later that night, the two of them went back to the hostel together. They were both very quiet. Bernard walked with Ikuko to her room. They stood outside while she looked for her key. Then, for a moment, they looked at one another. She remembered how he had held her as the van had crashed into them. 'Thank you, Bernard,' she said.

'Will you be all right now?' he asked.

'Yes,' said Ikuko. 'Yes, thanks.' She went into her room. She listened to Bernard's steps as he walked away and then sat on her bed for a time. 'Maybe I should phone Hiroshi,' she thought. Then she remembered Bernard had her phone.

She decided to have a bath and lay for a long time in the hot water. It wasn't until she was putting her clothes back on that she realised something was missing. The ring wasn't on her finger. 'Maybe I lost it when we crashed,' she thought. But it didn't seem to matter.

She sat in her room, thinking about the day, wondering about Mike. She still felt shaky. Then there were steps outside and a knock on the door. She opened it. Bernard stood there, holding her mobile phone. He gave it back to her. 'I rang the hospital about Mike. They said he's awake now and he seems OK. He's going to have to stay in a few days, but he's going to be all right.'

Suddenly Ikuko found it all too much. She turned away from the door and started to cry. Then she felt Bernard's arms round her. 'Ikuko. It's all right. It's all fine.' They stayed like that for a long time until she stopped crying. She realised that she wanted to stay like this, close to him.

# Chapter 6
# Telling the truth

The light shone brightly through the thin curtains in Ikuko's bedroom. It was Sunday morning. There was a knock on the door. Lucretia's voice called, 'Are you all right? We all heard what happened. Shall I bring you some breakfast?'

'Yes, I'm all right. I'm fine. But I don't want any breakfast, thanks.' Ikuko didn't open the door.

She turned to Bernard and said softly, 'I have to talk to you...There are things I need to tell you.'

'Me, too...I have a lot to tell you. But we have time.'

Ikuko got out of bed and pulled back her curtains. Light filled the room. The street outside was white, covered in snow. The sky was blue and the sun shone. 'Come on,' said Bernard. 'Let's go for a walk. Then we can talk.'

It was difficult to walk in the snow. Ikuko held on to Bernard's arm. The air was cold but the wind had gone. It was quiet. Only a few cars drove slowly down the road leaving black pathways in the snow.

'Bernard...I don't know what happened to me. I've already got a boyfriend in Japan.'

'Yes, I know. Do you want to tell me about him?'

'He's called Hiroshi. We've been together for two years. He's my first real boyfriend. We're getting married later this year. But I wanted to travel first, to see new places. He didn't mind at all. He trusted me...'

'Have you told him anything yet?' Bernard asked.

'No,' she replied. 'I thought maybe there was nothing to tell. Until last night.'

'Ikuko, there are things I have to tell you, too.' Bernard stopped and took out a small photograph from his wallet. He passed it to Ikuko. Two African children with round eyes and serious faces stared out of it. Ikuko looked at the photo and then at Bernard. She didn't say anything.

After a minute, Bernard said, 'This is Beatrice. She's eleven. Chiole is five.' He pointed to each girl as he spoke.

Finally, Ikuko found the words. 'So you're married?'

'I got married twelve years ago. I was very young. We were both very young. Too young.'

'So what happened?' Ikuko asked.

'She left me. She went back to Lusaka, to the capital, where her people live, and left me and the children.'

'And...what happened to the children?'

'I brought them up on my own,' Bernard answered. 'It wasn't easy. My mother helped at first, but now she's getting old. So when I got the chance to study in England, I asked my wife to come back to Mungwi while I was away. Just for a year. To look after the children.'

They stood there for a minute. Ikuko wanted to ask Bernard why he hadn't told her before. But she didn't. She gave him back the photograph.

'They're lovely. Lovely children,' she said.

'Yes,' he said, as he put the photograph away, 'I miss them very much.' They started to walk again, side by side, but not touching.

'Maybe we shouldn't see each other any more,' Ikuko said. She looked down at her feet in the snow which was already changing to dirty grey water.

'I'm sorry about last night,' said Bernard.

Ikuko suddenly felt angry. 'Is that true? Are you really sorry?'

'No, Ikuko. I'm sorry I didn't explain before. I'll understand if you don't want to see me again. But I'm not sorry it happened.'

Ikuko thought about the last few weeks. Then she stopped and looked at him. 'No, I'm not sorry it happened either,' she said. 'And I still want to see you.'

Late that evening Ikuko sat alone in her room, holding her mobile phone. She took a deep breath and pressed the memory button. Hiroshi's number.

It was morning in Japan. Hiroshi was just getting up. It wasn't an easy conversation. She told him about the accident first.

'I was nearly thrown out of my seat. But the person sitting next to me, Bernard, he saved me.'

'Bernard? Is he English?' Hiroshi asked quickly.

She had forgotten how well Hiroshi knew her. How he could tell at once when something was important to her.

'No, he's Zambian,' Ikuko answered.

'What?' said Hiroshi.

'From Africa.'

'And he's your boyfriend? Tell me.'

'Yes,' Ikuko said slowly. 'Yes, I suppose so. I don't really know what's going to happen. I'm so sorry, Hiroshi.'

She had never seen Hiroshi angry, but she could tell he was angry now. 'You promised. I've waited for you,' he shouted. 'But I knew something was happening. I knew you weren't the same. What am I supposed to do now?'

'Oh, Hiroshi. I'm sorry. I'm sorry.' But he'd rung off.

She sat there for a moment not knowing what to do. Then she got out her diary. Maybe if she wrote everything down she'd feel clearer. She took out her pen and started. An hour later she was still writing.

*I don't understand how I feel about Bernard, but ever since I met him it's felt like a door opening – so many new ideas, new experiences. We're so happy together. I feel very bad about Hiroshi. But I can't help it. I thought I loved him. I trusted him, and he trusted me. But he wants a quiet life, a safe life, at home in Japan. I don't think I can live that life. Not yet, anyway. I don't know what will happen, but I'm happy I came to England.*

# Chapter 7
# News from Zambia

It was a windy Sunday afternoon at the end of March. Bernard and Ikuko were sitting in Bernard's room. Ikuko was reading an English newspaper, sometimes stopping to look words up in her dictionary. Bernard was writing an essay and there were books and papers all over the floor. A CD was playing, the music filling the room and going through the open window into the spring air.

Japan seemed a long way from this room filled with African music. Ikuko had written to Hiroshi to try to explain more about what had happened. After a while she'd received a letter back from him.

*I still think of you and hope you won't get hurt. I wish you'd come back to Japan. Then we could talk about this properly. But in the end you have to decide what you want.*

There was a knock on the door. 'Come in,' called

Bernard. Lucretia put her head round the door. 'Hello. There's a fax for you, Bernard. It was at reception. I brought it up. Here.' She handed him the paper and then left.

Bernard read the few handwritten lines. Then he looked up, his face serious. 'It's from Beatrice. My wife has gone back to Lusaka. She's left Beatrice and Chiole on their own.'

He was silent for a minute, thinking. Then he went on: 'Ikuko, I have to go back. They're too young to look after themselves. My mother and father are old and ill. There's no-one else.'

'What about your course...and us?' Ikuko asked.

'I don't know. But Ikuko, this can't be the end for us. We have to see each other again. But I don't know how.'

Three days later, Ikuko stood with Bernard at Heathrow Airport. Ikuko remembered the last time she had said goodbye in an airport – in Japan. What had happened to the promises she'd made Hiroshi then? She'd meant them at the time. She shivered, feeling suddenly cold. Bernard put his arm round her.

'I'll fax you as soon as I arrive in Mungwi,' he said. 'The phone's not so good for international calls. And you've got my school address – you can always write to me there. Remember, Ikuko, we'll be together again soon, somewhere.' For the last time Ikuko felt Bernard's arms round her.

'I'll see you soon,' she managed to say. And watched as his red jacket disappeared.

* * *

*4 May 2000*

*Just a month since Bernard left. And still no news. Nothing. No letter, no fax, no phone call. I can't believe that he doesn't care, that he's forgotten me. I can't forget him.*

Ikuko sat alone in her room looking out of the window. The trees were green now, not a fresh new green but already looking dark. There was nothing else to write. She'd done nothing special that day. Gone to classes but not learnt anything. She knew her teachers and friends were worried about her. In the last month she'd slept badly. Her face looked thin and even paler than usual. She'd written to Hiroshi – a short letter telling him that Bernard had gone home, but not saying any more than that.

She'd tried to fax Bernard, but the number he'd

given her didn't work. And she'd sent letter after letter, but there was no reply. She lay awake at night for hours thinking the same thoughts over and over again. 'Was I really stupid? Didn't I mean anything to him? Maybe he's back with his wife. Or with someone else. But why hasn't he told me?'

Then the mobile phone on the desk beside her rang. She picked it up, her heart racing.

'Ikuko. How are you?' It was Hiroshi.

'I'm all right. How are you? Did you get my letter?'

'Yes.' He paused. 'So what are you doing now?'

'Studying...nothing much,' Ikuko answered.

'Are you still planning to stay until July?' Hiroshi asked.

'I don't know. I haven't thought about it,' she said.

'Ikuko – come back to Japan. Come back here. I'll meet you at the airport. It would be better...'

'Maybe you're right. I'll think about it. Thanks, Hiroshi.' She put down her phone slowly. It had been good to talk to him, good to talk in her own language to someone who knew the old Ikuko. Maybe he was right. Maybe it was time to go home.

She opened her wardrobe and pulled out the blue suitcase.

# Chapter 8 Waiting

Ikuko and Hiroshi walked slowly together beneath the cherry trees in the park at Ome. The trees had finished flowering and it was already summer. Ikuko had been back a month, but she and Hiroshi were still careful with each other. She knew she had hurt him badly and that he wasn't sure what to do. Ikuko hadn't talked about her feelings for Bernard, and Hiroshi hadn't asked her any questions.

'Would you like to stop here?' asked Hiroshi. There was an empty seat under a tree. The Sunday afternoon crowds filled the park. Next to them, a young couple sat with their baby. She saw Hiroshi watching the baby, his hair falling over his eyes as usual. He would be such a good father, she thought. And she couldn't expect him to wait for her until she decided on her own feelings.

She wasn't even sure how she felt any more. She still couldn't forget Bernard. She had almost stopped expecting to hear from him, but part of her couldn't stop hoping. She had left her address at the hostel, and every morning she waited for the post to arrive. But there was no letter from England or from Zambia.

The next morning Ikuko lay in bed trying to make herself get up. 'But what for?' she thought. She had nothing to do that day. Except look for a job – and she knew she wouldn't do that.

She went and made herself a cup of coffee and sat drinking it. Then the post arrived. One letter. A letter in an airmail envelope. With Zambian stamps. A letter addressed to her in Birmingham and readdressed to Japan.

She sat and looked at the envelope, turning it over and over. She wondered what she expected to find inside. She opened it and started to read.

*Dear Ikuko,*

*I've just received a letter from you although I don't think it was your first letter. It took a long time to arrive. They had sent it to the wrong school, and no-one sent it on. And the fax at school is broken. We're waiting for a new part but it hasn't come yet. They say it should arrive by the end of the month, then you can fax me.*

*I've written to you many times, but I don't think*

*you've received my letters either. I gave the letters to a driver to post in Lusaka so that they'd get to you more quickly. But maybe he didn't post them. So now I'll post my letters from Mungwi.*

*It is a good thing I came back. The children were staying with my parents, but my mother was very ill and two weeks after I came back she died. It has been a very sad time for all of us. Now I can't leave the children. I can't come back to England. My wife has met someone else and she wants to divorce me. But it will take time.*

*Ikuko, I left in such a hurry. Maybe now you're tired of waiting for me. Soon you'll be going back to Japan. Maybe it would be better for you to forget about me. Maybe it's better for you to marry someone from your own country, instead of being with a man who can't marry you yet, who lives such a different life.*

*But I'm missing you very much. I can't leave Zambia – but can you come here? I don't know if this life would ever be possible for you, but when I sit with the children in the evening, I wish you were here with us. Please, if you still want to see me, if there's any chance, try to come to Zambia. Please come. I'll be here.*

*Love from,*
*Bernard*

She looked at the date at the top of the letter: 10 May. The day she'd left England. It was nearly three months since she'd seen Bernard.

She found a sheet of paper and started to write a fax.

# Chapter 9
# African sunshine, African rain

A chicken hurried across the ground as a young Zambian girl in school clothes, carrying a bag of books, walked into the backyard. It was nearly five o'clock, but the September sun was still hot, shining on the cooking pots and pans left out to dry. At the far end of the yard there was a big mango tree with wide green leaves and small green fruit. The girl walked towards the back door and dropped her bag on the table just outside it. The house had just one floor, with the door in the middle and a window on each side.

'Ikuko, I'm home!' the girl called.

Ikuko came out into the hot sun. She looked very different from the pale unhappy girl who had opened Bernard's letter months earlier. Her face was relaxed and happy. Holding on to her other hand was a little girl with dark skin and wide eyes.

'Hello, Beatrice. How was school?' Ikuko asked.

'It was good,' Beatrice replied in English. Then

Beatrice and the little girl spoke for a minute in Bemba, their own language. She turned to Ikuko again. 'Chiole says that today you went to the market. And you bought some tomatoes and onions.'

Ikuko laughed. 'Yes, she helped me choose them. Good ones!'

'Is my father back yet?' Beatrice asked.

'No, he's at his photography business. He'll be back soon, then we'll have dinner,' said Ikuko.

'What's for dinner?'

'Chicken and *nshima*. And salad,' answered Ikuko.

'I can make the *nshima* if you want,' said Beatrice. 'It's difficult for you. I can't imagine how you can live in Japan without eating *nshima*.'

Ikuko just smiled. She didn't want to tell Beatrice that she found it difficult to eat the heavy *nshima*. Flour and water cooked in a pan over the fire. But the children loved it and so did Bernard.

She had been in Zambia for almost four weeks. In some ways they had been the happiest weeks of her life. She had arrived at the small airport feeling frightened. Would she even recognise him? What would she do if he wasn't there to meet her? But he was there, smiling his crooked smile, looking just the same – except that in the hot sun he didn't need the red jacket. He had borrowed a friend's car and they drove from the airport to his house down the narrow roads, between low hills and trees. Everything was dry and dusty.

'Wait until the rains come next month,' Bernard said. 'Everything will be green. The grass will be higher than the houses.' Ikuko couldn't imagine rain as she looked up at the blue sky. So much space, she thought. The sky seemed wider than anywhere else she'd been.

They arrived at a square house. The two children came shyly out to meet them. Little Chiole just stood and stared with her thumb in her mouth. 'She doesn't know much English yet,' said Bernard.

Four weeks later, Ikuko and Chiole still couldn't say much to each other. But the little girl seemed to trust her. They spent a lot of time together while Bernard and Beatrice were at school. Ikuko found that all the housework took a long time – cleaning and cooking, washing and ironing. The house had electric light, there was a fridge and a television, but no washing machine or electric cooker.

Every day she walked to the market with Chiole and bought vegetables. It was a long walk there and back in the hot sun, carrying the heavy bag of vegetables. She watched the African women with their babies on their backs and their shopping on their heads. It looked easy, but Ikuko had tried and couldn't do it. When they got back she was hot and tired. Then it was good to sit on the seat by the back door watching Chiole play in the garden.

She was always happy when Bernard arrived home, although often it was very late. He had started up his photography business, so he went straight there after school. It was doing well and he had a lot of work to do in the evenings. But eventually he would arrive, and they would all eat outside together in the cool evening air, with the sound of the insects in the dark and the stars shining above, before the children went sleepily to bed.

They hadn't made any decisions about the future yet. 'Wait and see,' said Bernard. 'Zambia isn't like England or Japan. I'd like you to stay, but you must decide for yourself.'

All through the next week it got hotter and hotter. The daily walk to the market was even more tiring. Little Chiole lay on her bed most of the day. Everyone seemed hot and tired.

'It's a difficult time, the end of the hot season,' said Bernard. 'It'll be better when the rains come.'

And the next afternoon the rains came. First the wind arrived, blowing the dust across the yard. Then big drops of water landed on the hot dry ground. The smell was wonderful and Chiole ran about laughing and shouting.

By evening it was still raining and the yard outside was wet and muddy. Beatrice and Bernard came home with their clothes wet through. 'It's early for the rains,' said Bernard. 'It'll probably not last long. But it's good to be cool again.'

The next morning was fine, but in the afternoon the rain started again. That evening Ikuko found that the little house seemed to be full of wet clothes and muddy children. She realised how much of their life they usually lived outside, at the big table by the back door. Now they ate their dinner indoors without speaking – it was difficult to talk with the noise of the rain and thunder. Suddenly there was a bang and all the lights went out. 'Don't worry,' said Bernard. 'It's just an electricity cut. Beatrice, get the candles and then go to bed.'

Bernard and Ikuko sat without speaking in the

candle light as the storm went away. But it wasn't an easy silence. It was the silence of two people trying to decide what to say to each other.

Then Ikuko spoke. 'Bernard, I love you very much. And I love your children, too. I'd like to stay here. But I don't know if I can.'

'I know, Ikuko. I wanted you to come here, to see what it was like. But I know it isn't an easy life for you.'

'I don't think it's that. It's been a bit difficult since the rains came, but it's not that. But, Bernard, wherever I am I want to be somewhere else. What's wrong with me? Why can't I be happy with what I've got?'

'You're looking for something, Ikuko. But you don't know what. Maybe you'll find it back in Japan after all. In your own country.'

'But if I leave who will look after the children?'

'I'll have to manage,' said Bernard. 'It won't be easy, but I can do it. That's not the problem. The problem is losing you. I hoped we'd stay together. But Mungwi isn't Tokyo. I couldn't live all my life in Birmingham, even though I loved it. And I don't think you can live in Mungwi, even though you've tried so hard.'

Their conversation continued as the candle burnt

down. At last the rain stopped. 'Let's go and sit outside on the bench,' said Bernard. They went out and sat on the wooden seat by the back door. The clouds had gone and the big African moon was full and bright. Ikuko reached out and took Bernard's hand.

'I think I have to go. I think in the end I belong in Japan. But a part of me will always be here. And I'm happy I came. I'm happy I have these memories of our time together. Maybe we'll never meet again, but in a way we'll always be together because we'll both remember these times.'

* * *

It had rained that morning, but now the sun shone on the pools of water in the yard. Ikuko sat on the bench outside the house with her blue suitcase next to her. Beatrice and Chiole were outside at the front, waiting for Bernard's friend to arrive with the car.

Bernard came out through the back door. He stood there, looking at her. 'Stay there a minute,' he said, and went inside. He came back with his camera. The Japanese girl looked back at him, unsmiling, as the camera clicked and recorded that second for the years to come.

# PART 2
# COMING HOME

# Chapter 10
# Plane to Egypt

The hot Egyptian sun shone down on the new Red Sea Research and Tourist Centre. It shone on the low white buildings, the blue sea next to them and the green air-taxi park. It was the year 2050. Tiny air-taxis, looking like insects in the sky, flew here and there, taking passengers to beaches along the coast or to the airport at Marsa Alam.

In the research centre, a well-dressed woman with a young face and white hair was talking to a screen on the wall. She looked Arabic, but her English had no accent.

'OK, Joyce. Well, as you know, the opening ceremony begins at eleven o'clock and your presentation will follow the President's talk. So, we'll see you in an hour? Good. Fine. Bye, then.' The screen went black and the woman turned round.

On the other side of the room two men looked up from the papers they'd been studying.

'Was that Joyce Mutanga?' asked Sven, the taller of the two. He had very blond hair and a Swedish accent.' She doesn't believe in arriving early, does she, Fatima?'

Fatima was calm as always. 'She called to say they've just arrived at Marsa Alam, so she'll be here in ten minutes.'

The second man looked annoyed. He was Japanese, with a pointed chin and his hair long above his dark eyes but, like the others, he spoke in English. 'Nice of her to let us know,' he said crossly. 'Just an hour before the opening. Why on earth didn't she call earlier?'

Fatima laughed. 'You never know with Joyce, Taka. It's no good getting cross. She's just like that. But I'm pleased she agreed to speak. I don't think this centre would be here if she hadn't done so much to let people know about the type of research we're doing. She's really an excellent media-scientist, one of the best in the world, even if you don't like her as a person.'

'I'm looking forward to meeting her,' said Sven. 'She's African, isn't she?'

'I think so – though I don't know if she's ever actually lived in Africa,' replied Fatima. 'She lives in Australia now, in Sydney. I think she's spent most of her life there.'

'She sounds amazing,' said Sven. 'Those presentations of hers are so beautiful, you don't realise how much research has gone into them. And she's only...what? Thirty?'

'Twenty-nine,' said Fatima. 'Yes, you're right, Sven. She's brilliant – she lives for the sea and for her filming. It's strange though. She knows how to talk to people through her films, but when you meet her she's actually very hard to talk to. She doesn't seem interested in people at all.'

The Japanese man still looked cross. 'I met her last year in the Ryūkyū Islands when I worked there. She came down to do some underwater filming. We were looking forward to meeting her. We arranged a party for her, but she only stayed ten minutes. We hardly saw her the whole time she was with us. She just went off on her own – didn't really talk to anyone. I remember her...Beautiful but selfish, I thought. Cold.' He shook his head at the memory.

'Well, I'm happy she's here – cold or not,' said Fatima.

As the supersonic plane landed at Marsa Alam, Joyce Mutanga turned off the video-disk that she wore round her neck and stretched out her long brown legs. She would be happy to get out of the plane, but she wasn't looking forward to the next few hours.

She'd agreed to speak at the opening ceremony because she was interested in the work that Fatima and her team were doing. But even though she had worked in media all her life, she'd never got used to the public. She didn't mind doing the presentation – talking to the hundreds of people in front of her and the millions watching her on TV. She knew she could talk confidently about her work. It was what came before and after that she didn't enjoy. Being polite to people she didn't know, people who only wanted to talk to her because she was famous. Never mind. It would soon be over. The next day she'd be on her way back to Sydney.

She made her way off the plane and straight to the air-taxi. Back in Africa, she thought, looking down at the dry land. But a long way from home.

Joyce's name was known by people all over the world who were interested in studying the life of the seas. But she'd been born in the middle of Africa, in a country which had no coast, where fish were things found in the freezer in supermarkets or sold dried in the markets. As a small child she used to go to the market with her mother and father when they were all still living together, and her mother used to buy the tiny dried fish for dinner. But she'd never seen fish alive and swimming. She'd never seen the sea.

But then everything changed. Her mother moved to Australia to start a new life and, at the age of eight, Joyce joined her. She stood on the beach at Sydney, her African life behind her, and watched the waves crashing on the sand.

'I want to go in,' she'd said to her mother. Her mother had just laughed. But Joyce's school had a swimming pool and in six months she was as confident in water as on land.

She soon moved from the swimming pool to the sea and when she was twelve she did her first underwater dive. A new artificial gill, which allowed divers to take oxygen from the water instead of from a heavy scuba-tank, was just being introduced. Joyce was excited by the freedom it gave her to discover an underwater world where fish were not frozen or dried, but alive and in their own place.

'It's like flying,' she said to her mother. 'You've got no weight. You're completely free. And on your own.'

She started to make videos of what she saw, using a cheap underwater camera. Back at home, she used her computer to add words and music. Her mother worried about her. 'You're fifteen,' she said. 'You should be enjoying yourself. Going to parties. Making friends.'

But Joyce didn't like parties and didn't seem to need friends. By the time she was eighteen, and ready to begin her course in Media and Maritime Studies at the University of Sydney, she was already well known. Her work was on the Internet and she was in touch with marine scientists all over the world. She had found something that filled her life and that she was good at. It was all she wanted, she thought.

# Chapter 11
# Swimming alone

For the audience in the big central hall, it was like being deep under the sea, moving through blue waters. Wherever they looked – the walls, the floor, the ceiling –seemed to be water. Joyce's voice spoke softly, but clearly, over the music. 'And that's why I believe that this project is only a beginning. We must understand that the plants and fish of the sea live with us, not for us. We must work to make sure that we never lose this richness and beauty.'

As Joyce ended her presentation, the water disappeared and the walls and ceiling became white again. For a moment there was silence, then the room was filled with the sound of applause. Of all the presentations, this would be the one everyone would remember. Joyce stood, waiting for the applause to stop. She smiled once and then her face was serious again.

Sven whispered, 'That was wonderful. Brilliant.'

Taka nodded. 'Yes,' he said, pushing the dark hair out of his eyes. 'Not bad at all.'

Joyce was certainly a good speaker. Taka watched her step down from the platform and move towards the door.

'Come on, Sven,' Taka said.

Sven and Taka followed the crowd towards the reception hall, which was built out into the sea. One wall was completely made of glass and beyond it tiny fish swam between pieces of pink and orange coral. Joyce stood among a group of people. She wasn't saying much and she didn't look happy. Sven walked straight up to her.

'Hello. I'm Sven Berger from Sweden,' he said. 'I'm one of the team here in the Red Sea Centre. Can I just say how much I enjoyed your presentation and how much I like your work?'

Joyce looked back at him, unsmiling. 'Thank you.' She didn't say any more.

'Are you staying here long?' Sven continued. 'I've been trying to develop a new type of underwater film. I wanted to ask your opinion about it.'

'No,' said Joyce. 'No, I don't think I'll have time.' Sven realised she wasn't looking at him at all, but looking over his shoulder. The silence became difficult and he felt better when he saw Taka coming towards them.

'Hello. I'm Taka,' he said, smiling politely at Joyce. 'I believe we've met before.'

'Have we?' she asked.

'When you came to the Ryūkyū Islands last year.'

'Oh,' she replied. 'I'm afraid I don't remember you. Anyway, if you'll excuse me, I have to go now.' She turned and walked away towards the door.

Taka and Sven looked at one another, their eyebrows raised. 'She might be a famous media-scientist, but it's time she learned to be polite,' said Taka angrily.

'Cool it, Taka. She's not interested in anyone except herself. And her work. So what? Come on, let's get a drink. We're supposed to be having a good time.'

Joyce left the room, trying to keep her face calm. She knew she'd made that Japanese man angry. But why should she remember everyone she met? She was introduced to so many people all over the world. And she never could remember faces. Or names. Except the names of fish.

She went back to her hotel next to the Centre but she couldn't relax. It was four o'clock and she had all the evening ahead of her. She wondered if she could leave now. But it would be sad to go without taking a look at the sea. She changed into her swimming things, put on a skirt, picked up her artificial gill and left the room.

She was just passing reception when she heard her name. 'Joyce! Hi...are you going out?'

It was Fatima. Joyce didn't know what to say. She didn't want Fatima to come with her.

'I thought I'd go for a walk,' she said at last.

'Is that your gill? Were you hoping for a swim?' asked Fatima.

'Yes...maybe a quick one. Is there anywhere near here swimmers can go?'

'There's a beach just down the coast the project people use. I'll fly you down in the micro-plane if you want.'

'I don't want to be any trouble. You must be busy,' said Joyce.

'Oh, it's no trouble. I've booked a meal for the project team at a restaurant just by the beach there – just the three of us. We were hoping you'd join us. We're meeting at seven. It won't take me a minute to drop you there now, and you can join us at the restaurant after your swim.'

Joyce seemed to have no choice. 'Thank you,' she said, and followed Fatima out of the door.

The little plane quietly landed on the sand in the middle of an empty beach.

Fatima turned to Joyce. 'I'll drop you here – this is a good place. The restaurant's only ten minutes' walk away. It's five now, so you've got plenty of time before we meet at seven. You're happy swimming on your own?'

'Yes, thanks,' Joyce said and got out, closing the door behind her.

Joyce sat on the beach for a long time, feeling the late afternoon sun warm on her shoulders. Then, as the sun got lower, she walked down the beach, holding her gill. At the water's edge she stopped and looked down at her feet. In her hurry to leave the hotel, she'd forgotten the bag with her flippers. 'Stupid of me,' she thought. She was a strong swimmer, but it would be difficult to swim far without flippers on her feet. Well, she'd have a short swim since she was here. She had light tennis shoes on, but the beach here was clear and sandy. She decided to keep her shoes on in case there were rocks later on.

The water was warm at first around her legs, then grew cooler as the sea got deeper. She could see her white tennis shoes shining on the yellow sand under the water. When the water was deep enough, she pulled the mask down over her face, turned on her artificial gill and dived under. Suddenly, she was in a new world. The sand danced below her and the sunlight shone through the waves making patterns. Then rocks started to appear in the sand. The small coloured fish who lived among the rocks swam so close to Joyce that she could almost touch them.

Surprisingly quickly, she got to the reef and swam along slowly until she found a place where there was a break. She swam out to the edge. She guessed that the drop below her to the bottom of the sea was at least thirty metres, maybe more. But it was far less frightening than the busy reception hall full of people. She didn't go down deep, but swam along the side of the reef, pausing every now and then to look at the fish and plants that lived there.

When she realised that it was getting hard to see, she swam back up to the surface. She realised she had been down much longer than she'd thought – the sun was low over the hills. At least she wouldn't have to spend very long in the restaurant.

Without her flippers it took her a long time to swim back along the reef. By the time she reached the break in the reef it was nearly dark. She swam back towards the land, raising her head above the water now and then to check she was swimming in the right direction. The sun had gone down now, but there was still a line of light behind the hills in front of her. She couldn't see the sand beneath her, but when she put her feet down they touched the ground. She stood up to walk the last few metres to the edge of the sea. The evening wind against her wet body made her shiver.

The water was only just above her knees now. She took another step forward and almost fell as her foot hit something under the water. Then she screamed, again and again.

# Chapter 12
# Stonefish

'I thought she'd be here by now,' said Fatima.

Fatima, Sven and Taka were sitting in the restaurant together, looking out over the water. The sun had almost set and the moon was rising over the sea, round and full.

'I expect she's just gone back to the Centre without telling you,' said Taka.

'But how could she have got back? It's too far to walk,' said Fatima. She was worried. Perhaps she shouldn't have left Joyce there on her own. 'Maybe I should...'

Then they heard a sound from far away across the dark beach.

'What's that?' asked Sven. They heard it again. Someone was screaming. Sven and Fatima looked at one another.

'We'll take the plane,' said Fatima. 'We might need it. And it's got lights.'

But Taka was already out of his seat and running. He could only hear the sound of his own breath.

He was a good runner but the sea was almost three hundred metres away and the soft sand made running difficult. But he knew that every second might count.

He had almost run past Joyce in the dark when he heard her crying. She was sitting half in and half out of the water, holding one leg.

'Joyce. What's happened?' he asked.

But she didn't seem to hear him. He bent over her and tried to lift her to her feet but she screamed. Very carefully, he picked her up in his arms and carried her a little way up the beach, then laid her down on the sand. He got down beside her. In the moonlight he could see that there was dark blood on the white shoe on her left foot. He felt the bottom of the shoe gently. There were four round holes. He suddenly felt frightened and angry.

'You've stepped on a stonefish,' he said. 'You know all about the sea, and then you go out in shoes like this. Why weren't you more careful?'

Joyce didn't reply. Her eyes were closed and her whole body was shaking. Taka took off her shoe. Her foot was already starting to get bigger and he could see the four dark marks where the sharp poisonous spines on the stonefish's back had gone deep into her foot. Taka felt her leg. The poison was already moving upwards. He spoke more to himself than to Joyce now.

'Four holes. That's a lot of poison. She could lose the leg – or worse. It needs something doing to it – fast. Where the hell are the other two?'

There was a low humming sound over by the restaurant. He looked up and saw a light coming nearer, about five metres above the ground. It landed on the soft sand a few metres away. Fatima called out of the window. 'What's the matter? What's happened?'

'It's Joyce. She's stepped on a stonefish,' said Taka. 'We need to do something for her now, then get her to hospital. Is there a medical pack in the plane?'

'Yes – under your seat, Sven – but I don't know if there's anything for stonefish.'

Sven got out, holding a red box. Taka opened it. 'Good. OK, there's some useful stuff here...If I give her this, it should do something about the poison.' He took out a small plastic bottle and checked it carefully, then opened up one end. He held the bottle against Joyce's foot and pressed a small button. She didn't move.

'That should stop the poison. Now she needs to get to hospital fast.'

He picked her up and carried her to the plane, laying her carefully in the back. There was one place left in the front. 'Do you want to come with us, Taka?'

asked Fatima.

'No,' said Taka. 'You two go. I need a walk. And a drink. She'll be OK with you.'

And as the little plane disappeared in the sky Taka walked across the moonlit beach back to the restaurant. 'Why wasn't she more careful?' he asked himself again. But he felt more unhappy than angry.

# Chapter 13
# White shoes

Joyce didn't know where she was. In her mind, confused by the poison from the stonefish and the drugs, she felt as though she was back underwater, but the water was very warm. Too warm...In fact it was almost burning her...Or maybe she had been out in the sun too long. You had to be careful with the sun in the hot season in Africa. She needed something to drink – she was very thirsty.

'Mother!' she called. 'Father!'

They couldn't be far away. Why had they put her to bed? Joyce decided to get up. She looked down... She was wearing her best dress, the one she had been given for her sixth birthday. And her new white shoes. But there was a problem with her shoes...she couldn't remember what. She'd done something to them and her father was angry with her. And her foot hurt, her foot and her leg. Maybe the white shoes were hurting her.

'Father,' she heard herself crying.

She tried to get up but when she moved her leg

the pain made her stop. She knew that something was wrong. She lay in the hospital bed, the sheet white against her skin, living again that last day in the small house in Zambia.

She'd gone out playing in her new white shoes. It was the rainy season and the road was muddy. She'd been playing with her friends and got red mud all over her shoes. She tried to wash them in a small pool of water by the road, but they just looked worse.

When she got home her father shouted at Joyce. 'Your new shoes! Why weren't you more careful?' And then her mother came in and started shouting at her father. They didn't notice the little girl go to her bedroom. They didn't hear her crying herself to sleep.

In the morning her father had gone to work. But her mother had packed a suitcase and the two of them had travelled all day in the bus along the muddy road, back to Mungwi and her grandfather's house. She never saw her father again.

Joyce opened her eyes and said to the doctor bending over her, 'Are you angry? About my shoes?'

'No-one's angry,' said the doctor. Joyce stared for a minute. 'Who are you? You're not my father,' she said.

'I'm a doctor. You stepped on a stonefish. You're

going to be all right.' He looked at the computer screen next to her bed. 'You need to rest. I'm giving you some drugs to help you to sleep. When you wake up you'll feel better, and you can see your friends. OK?'

'No...I don't want to see anyone,' said Joyce. She still felt confused, felt that in some way she'd behaved badly. She fell back into a restless sleep again, with the pain still there under the drugs.

When she woke up again she was on her own. The sun was shining through the window of her small private room in the hospital. The clock on her silver video screen said nine o'clock. The pain in her leg was not as bad, but she had a headache and she was very thirsty.

The door opened and a woman came in with breakfast. Joyce wasn't hungry but she drank the orange juice. The sun moved around the walls of the hospital room. She slept a little. When she woke up there was a message on the computer screen next to her bed.

'Joyce, I do hope you're all right. Is there anything we can do for you? Call me any time, Fatima.'

But she didn't want to see Fatima.

A nurse looked in but Joyce kept her eyes shut

and she left. Confused memories came and went. Applause from an audience...a man's angry face... someone carrying her.

The next thing she knew there were quick steps outside in the corridor. They stopped for a moment. Then the door opened. Joyce still didn't open her eyes.

'Joyce?'

It was a voice she knew, a man's voice. She suddenly remembered the pain in the water. How someone had picked her up...She remembered this voice, soft but angry.

'Yes...I should have been careful,' she said.

She opened her eyes and saw Taka's face.

# Chapter 14 The visit

Taka stood by the bed looking down at her lying there, her dark eyes very big in her brown face, her hands lying still on the white sheets. She suddenly looked very young to him, no longer the powerful woman who had made him so angry, but a frightened girl who had nearly died in the sea she loved.

'I'm sorry I said that,' he said. 'I thought you were going to die. I was frightened.'

Joyce closed her eyes. Taka saw two tears run down her cheeks. Without thinking, he reached out and took her hand.

'Joyce, you're OK. You're going to be fine.'

'I'm sorry. I don't know what the matter is. I've had dreams...' Her voice was quiet.

'I expect they've given you drugs. To stop the pain.'

'Yes,' she said.

'That's probably what's doing it. But you should be all right now. Do you want me to call anyone?'

'No. No-one.' Joyce closed her eyes.

'Are you tired? Do you want me to go?' Taka asked.

She was still for a minute, then she shook her head. 'No,' she said softly. 'Stay here for a bit.'

For a long time Taka sat by the bed, holding her hand. He wasn't sure if she was awake or asleep. Then she said softly, still with her eyes closed. 'Taka...what happened?'

'It was a stonefish,' he said.

He felt her hand hold his tighter. Then she opened her eyes and looked at him. 'I would have died, wouldn't I? If you hadn't been there.'

'You could have done.' He remembered the feel of her body, shivering with pain and cold, as he'd carried her out of the dark water.

She was quiet for a moment. She moved her leg under the covers, carefully.

'Does it still hurt?' he asked.

'Yes, but it's much better than it was. How long do you think I'll have to stay here?'

'Not long. I expect you'll be swimming again in a week,' he said, trying to be cheerful.

She bit her lip. Suddenly she looked tired.

'I'd better go,' said Taka. She nodded her head and he let go of her hand. He didn't want to leave her.

'I'll come back this evening if you want,' he offered.

She smiled and said, 'Yes, I'd like that.'

Taka left the room and Joyce lay there on her own again. She thought about her dream. The memory of that day in Zambia had been hidden very deep in her mind. It had needed the pain and the drugs to bring it back. Now she lay and thought about it all, the people who had been part of her life there, and what they had meant to her.

Taka left the hospital and came out into the hot air. He went back to the research building and sat in front of his computer for a few minutes. But he couldn't work. He typed Joyce's name into the computer and called up the recording of her presentation. He replayed the last few minutes when the lights came up and Joyce's face filled the screen. He looked at her dark head and long neck, the high cheekbones, the shy, crooked smile she gave as her talk ended. Then, not knowing quite why he did it, he copied the recording onto the video-disk he wore round his neck.

He stood up and moved around the room restlessly. Just then the video-disk round his neck beeped. A call. A white-haired Japanese woman was standing in a garden. She spoke to him in Japanese. 'Taka. You're looking very well,' she said.

'Grandmother!'

'But your hair needs cutting! You're just like your grandfather. Never time for a haircut. Hair falling into your eyes.'

Taka laughed. His grandmother and he had always been very close. Taka was her first grandchild and the only boy.

'I've been busy! We've just had the opening ceremony for the Centre,' he explained.

'Do you realise how long it is since you visited me? I think it's time you came. Take the weekend off. You work too hard! I'll see you on Saturday.' And his disk went dark again as she finished speaking.

# Chapter 15
# Night dive

That evening Joyce sat by the window in her room in the hospital. She had a thin plastic covering on her left foot. She looked out at the sea in the light of the setting sun. Only twenty-four hours ago she'd been swimming in that sea, feeling safe and at home in the water. She shivered, remembering the danger that the water had hidden.

She heard quick steps coming down the corridor, almost running, then the door opened. She knew who it would be and she was smiling as she turned around. 'Taka!' she said.

'How are you feeling?' he asked.

'Oh, OK. Fine, in fact.'

'Have you seen the doctor again?'

'Yes,' replied Joyce. 'He says I'm all right. He says I can leave tonight if I want. I can walk fine. A bit slow, but it doesn't hurt at all. It's amazing, isn't it? Only twenty-four hours. He says it's because you acted so quickly.'

'Oh,' said Taka. 'That's great.' But he didn't seem

sure. He paused for a minute. 'So where will you go now?'

'Home, I suppose,' said Joyce.

'Back to Sydney?' asked Taka.

Joyce thought of her tiny flat in Sydney where she stayed in between travelling. But was it her home?

'Yes, I suppose so,' she said quietly.

'Do you have family there?' Taka asked.

'No...well, my mother used to be there but she lives in the USA now.'

Taka paused, then spoke very fast. 'Why don't you stay for a day or two. I could show you some of the work we've been doing.'

Joyce looked up at him, uncertain. 'I...I'm not sure. Aren't you busy?'

'No, I've got some holiday to take. We could go swimming. You could stay with me.'

'No!' said Joyce, and saw Taka's eyes widen. 'Sorry, I meant...I don't want to go in the sea.'

She didn't know how to explain to him that the thought of the sea, the dark water, filled her with fear. That she felt as if she never wanted to go back there.

Taka looked at her. 'Did the doctor say you could swim?'

'Yes?' she said slowly.

'Right. We're going diving. Right now. You've got to get back into the sea – you've got to face this fear.'

Joyce looked out of the window. The sun had almost set. There were just lines of red in the west. 'I didn't say I was afraid.'

He looked at her. 'You didn't need to say it. I can see. I've been the same – once when my gill went wrong. The only thing to do is to face up to it straight away. But not on your own. We'll do this together.'

'But it's dark...' Joyce began.

'So we'll do a night dive,' Taka said as he jumped to his feet. 'Come on. Your gill's here. And I've got everything else we need. We'll tell the doctor on the way out.'

And Joyce found herself walking out of the door.

Half an hour later they were sitting in the micro-plane. Taka turned to her, smiling. 'It's ages since I've done a night dive. I suppose you've done lots?'

'Yes...but not for a long time.'

'We'll take a boat out to the reef. Then we can get straight to the deep water,' he said.

They landed behind the restaurant. Five minutes later they were sitting in a little boat moving quietly over the calm water. The moon was out, almost full, making a white path down the sea. In front of them a narrow line of white showed where the rocks of the reefs came up to the top of the water. Then they were through the break in the reef where she had swum the day before. Taka stopped the boat. He handed her a headband with a light on it, and put one around his own head. They put on their flippers and artificial gills.

'Ready?' he asked. Then he was over the side of the boat and in the water. The boat rocked and then was still again. Joyce put a hand over the side. The water was cold and dark. She thought of how far it went below them.

'I can't go in,' she said.

Taka looked at her from the water. 'You've got to come in, Joyce. You can do it.'

Joyce stood up. She waited a few seconds, unsure. Then, suddenly, she dived and was gone.

For a moment Taka was frightened. Then he saw a light moving up through the water towards him. Her head appeared, wet and shining.

'It's beautiful!' she said. 'Come on, Taka.' She took his hand.

Slowly they swam together, his pale body next to

her dark one. The coral shone red and purple, quite different from the daytime colours. Beautiful fish came out of their homes in the reef, attracted by the lights Joyce and Taka carried. Now and then Joyce would point at something: Taka's eyes would follow her finger and see some special fish or plant.

They came to the surface together. Taka turned off his torch and leaned over to turn off Joyce's. The full moon shone over them. The lights of the restaurant could be seen in the distance. But here they were on their own.

'Cold?' he asked her. She shook her head.

'I feel wonderful,' she said, smiling. 'Thank you, Taka.'

He reached out a hand to her and pulled her towards him. She came easily, her body weightless in the water. Then he kissed her and she tasted of the sea.

* * *

Less than an hour later they were at the restaurant. They sat outside looking over the dark water in the moonlight, waiting for their food to arrive.

'Do you often go back to Japan?' Joyce asked Taka.

'I haven't been back for a while. But I'm going on Saturday – to see my grandmother.'

'How old is she?' Joyce asked.

'Oh...about seventy. Not so old.'

'Are you close to her?'

'Yes...I'm her only grandson. She always wanted me to study and travel. I don't think she had a very exciting life – high school, college, company job. Once she was married she left work to have my mother and never went back. She and my grandfather live a quiet life. She speaks good English, though. She used to make me practise with her when I was young. I don't know how she learned it so well.'

'And your grandfather? Is he still alive?' asked Joyce.

Taka smiled. 'Yes. I'm supposed to look like him, but I can't see it. Everyone says so, though.'

'It must be nice. To be all together: parents, grandparents, children. I'd like that, I think.' Joyce looked suddenly lonely.

Taka reached out and took her hand. 'Joyce, have you thought any more about staying here? Do you have to go back to Sydney? Can't you stay a little longer?'

'Where would I stay?' she asked.

'Stay with me,' he said.

She shook her head. 'Taka,' she said, 'I...I'd like to.

But I don't think I can.' She paused, looking for words.

'I know. It's all been so sudden. But – ' Taka began.

'No, it's not that. It's that I'm not really used to staying with people. I don't think I'm any good at it. My mother wasn't, nor was my grandmother. They both ran away. When my mother left my father, she took me up to my grandfather's house. Then she left Zambia and got a job in Australia. She left me with my grandfather.'

'Were you very unhappy?' asked Taka, thinking of the little girl left on her own.

'No...not then. I missed my parents at first. But I was very happy with my grandfather.'

She told him about her life in those years, walking home to the little house from the primary school down the road with her friends, the red dust warm on her feet. Sitting with her grandfather outside the house at the back, doing her homework. Climbing the mango tree when no-one was looking and eating the sweet yellow fruit.

Then the letter had come from her mother. She had a good job in Australia. She had found a school for Joyce. She wanted her back.

'I cried and cried. I didn't want to go to Australia. I

didn't even know where it was. But I went. And then I found the sea. That seemed safe. It was always there.'

'Yes,' said Taka. He was beginning to understand. 'But what about your grandfather?' he asked.

'I really missed him. We used to write sometimes. Once a year or so. Paper letters. He didn't like other messages. He wouldn't use a video-disk. And I went to see him once or twice, just for a few days. But the last few years I've been so busy...Then I had a message from my aunt...my mother's younger sister. Just before I came here. He'd died. He was eighty.'

'I'm sorry,' said Taka.

'I hadn't even known he was ill,' Joyce continued. 'But I was thinking about him today when I was in the hospital. I think I want to go back. Just to see the place again.'

Taka was quiet for a long time. Joyce started to feel nervous. She'd never told anyone so much about herself before. She'd never met anyone she wanted to tell.

'Joyce, you must be tired. Come on. I'll take you back to your hotel,' Taka offered.

Soon afterwards they were walking into the hotel. Taka waited as Joyce went to get her room key. The receptionist gave it to her, then handed her something else. Joyce looked down at it for a minute, then came towards Taka.

'Look.' She gave it to him. It was a paper envelope, looking old and dirty as if many people had touched it. Joyce's Sydney address had been crossed out and it had been readdressed to the hotel in Egypt. On the back of the envelope there was a name and address: Bernard Chiluba, 42 Kasama Road, Mungwi, Northern Province, Zambia.

'Bernard Chiluba?'

'My grandfather. It's taken three weeks to get to me. He must have written it just before he died.'

He handed it back to her. She opened it slowly. A key fell from the envelope and dropped onto the floor. Taka bent down and picked it up. It was an old metal key. He held it while Joyce read the letter: a single page of handwriting. Then she handed the letter to him.

*Dear Joyce,*

*I wanted to write to you because I know it's time to say goodbye. I've had a long life and now I think it's been long enough. I hope that sometime you'll come back to Mungwi. My house is waiting for you. Here is a key. You'll find some boxes in your old bedroom. They're for you. Maybe you'll find something to look at there.*

*I hope the house will be a place where you can spend some of your time, and maybe bring your family when you have one. Your mother never found a place where she could be happy, and neither did your grandmother. I'm sorry I couldn't make a place for them. But I hope that you will find a place where you can stay, somewhere in this small world.*

*Love from,*
*Grandfather*

'I have to go,' said Joyce. 'I'll fly from here. I could be there by tomorrow. I'll ask about tickets now. I can fly direct to Lusaka, then change...'

Taka shook his head. 'Joyce, you can't do anything more tonight. You need to sleep. All this after the dive. I shouldn't have taken you out there tonight.'

She looked at him. 'I'm pleased you did.'

'I'll book your flight,' he said. 'I need to get my ticket for Japan anyway. I'll come and meet you here tomorrow morning. We can have breakfast together.'

# Chapter 16
# A white diary

In the end it was three days before they booked the tickets. Three days in which they spent long lazy hours in and out of the sea, returning to Taka's flat to shower off the salt and sand.

Until, on the third morning, Taka woke up and stretched, then said, 'Joyce. What day is it?'

Joyce opened her eyes. 'Does it matter?'

But Taka was already racing round the room. 'It's Friday. Grandmother. I promised her I'd be there tomorrow. Where's my video-disk? I need to get the tickets. Joyce, do you want to come with me?'

She laughed. 'No. Remember – I'm going to Mungwi.'

He stopped and came and sat on the bed next to her. 'But you'll come back? You won't just disappear? We haven't talked.'

'We've talked for three days,' she said.

'Yes, but not about what we're going to do next.'

'Don't worry,' Joyce said. 'Just book those flights.'

That evening Taka was halfway around the world

on the last part of his journey. He walked down the quiet road where his grandmother lived. The house was only two floors high and more than sixty years old. Very old for Japan. He walked up to the entrance and the door opened. He heard his grandmother's voice call, 'Taka, come on in. I'm in the living room.' She sat in her low chair, her white hair around a pale face that looked younger than she was.

'So you're here,' she said as he entered the room.

Taka put his hand up and pushed the hair out of his eyes.

'Well, you're still the same. Your hair's still too long. Just like your grandfather,' she continued.

'Where is grandfather?' Taka asked.

'Out. He'll be back soon. Anyway, tell me what you've been doing. You look very well. Relaxed.'

'Yes.' He wondered how much to tell his grandmother. How much she'd understand. She probably dreamed of a nice Japanese wife for her only grandson.

'So your research centre's open now? How did the opening go?'

'It went really well. We had the President there. And a good opening presentation by a Zambian researcher. A media-scientist. She does underwater films.'

His grandmother sat up a bit straighter. 'Zambian. That's interesting,' she said. 'I'd like to have seen that.'

'Well, if you're interested, I can show you the presentation. It's recorded on my video-disk.'

He turned on the video-disk and found the recording, then handed it to his grandmother. But she didn't seem interested in the sea-life. She moved on quickly to the last part, with the close-up of Joyce speaking. She paused the recording and looked more carefully. Taka looked over her shoulder. There was Joyce looking back, with the shy crooked smile he'd seen so often in the last few days.

'She's a lovely girl,' his grandmother said. 'What's her name?'

'Joyce. Joyce Mutanga.'

His grandmother looked at him. 'Funny, a Zambian woman doing research on sea-life. Zambia's not by the sea.'

He looked at her in surprise. He didn't know his grandmother had even heard of Zambia. 'She was brought up in Sydney,' he replied.

'Oh, so you know her?' his grandmother asked.

He wasn't sure what to say. But he wanted to tell his grandmother about this new person in his life.

'Yes,' he said, 'I know her.' And he told her the story of the last five days.

'So you see,' he finished, 'she's gone back to this village, to Mungwi. To the house where she lived with her grandfather. Then she'll call me and we'll meet up. I don't know where. It doesn't matter. But I'm sure we'll meet up.'

During the story Taka's grandmother had gone very quiet. 'I'm sorry about Bernard,' she said in a low voice when Taka had finished.

Taka looked at her, confused. Who was Bernard? Then he remembered it was the name on the envelope that Joyce had shown him. The name of Joyce's grandfather. But surely he hadn't told his grandmother that?

A moment later his grandmother got up and went to a cupboard. She reached inside, right to the back, and took out a small white book. Taka noticed her hands were shaking.

'Taka, I'd like you to have this,' she said. 'It's a diary I kept for a few months many years ago, before I married your grandfather. I've never shown it to anyone. I want you to read it. And maybe Joyce would like to read it, too. Now I'm feeling a bit tired. I think it's time for my rest.'

Taka took the diary. There was a name on the outside: Ikuko Kanazawa.

'Kanazawa?' he said.

'That was my name before I was married.' She closed her eyes.

He put the diary carefully in his bag and got up. His grandmother spoke again, her eyes still closed. 'Next time you come, bring Joyce Chiluba.'

'She's Joyce Mutanga, grandmother.'

'Never mind. Joyce from Mungwi.'

# Chapter 17
# A box of photographs

Joyce stopped the taxi in Mungwi at the corner of Kasama Road and got out. She wanted to make the last part of her journey on foot. She'd hardly recognised the centre of the village. Tall new buildings stood where the old market place had been, and the old school was now an Open Education Centre. But along her road things hadn't changed so much. The houses looked smaller than she remembered and the street was narrower, but she'd only been an eight-year-old girl.

It was the end of the rainy season and the road was dry. Joyce walked on to number 42. The curtains were closed. She took the metal key out of her bag and opened the front door.

She walked into the hot dark living room. Her grandfather's bedroom was off on the left, and the kitchen and her room were at the back. She opened the door into her grandfather's room. The bed was made and the curtains were closed. It was tidy, too tidy.

She shut the door quickly and went through to the room that had been hers and, before that, where her mother and aunt had slept when they were little girls. There were two narrow beds. Joyce sat on the bed that had been hers. She remembered the nights she'd lain there while her grandfather watched the old television in the living room or listened to music. No arguments, no shouting. Just her and her grandfather. She realised that here she felt at home. Was it the only place? She thought of the sunshine coming through the windows in Taka's flat. No, now there was somewhere else, someone else. But it was still good to be here.

She sat and looked around the room. Boxes were piled up in a corner, covered in dusty plastic. She pulled the plastic back and looked at them. Some were dated. The dates went back over sixty years. Joyce picked up as many of the boxes as she could carry, took them outside and sat on the old wooden bench behind the house.

It was a long bench – when she was a child she sometimes used to lie there and sleep in the hot afternoon. The bench had been very old even then. Joyce remembered how her grandfather had mended it when it had broken. Now, twenty years later, it was broken again. But it could be mended, thought Joyce. The mango tree still stood at the end of the yard, ready for little children to climb.

She put the dusty boxes on the seat beside her and cleaned her hands on her jeans. She opened one box. It was dated 2010. It was full of photographs: colour pictures of Mungwi brides and bridegrooms from forty years ago. They would be middle-aged now. Few of them would still be here in this small town – like her family, they would be living all over Africa, all over the world.

She looked at the dates on the other boxes: 2012, 2007, 2002. One box was undated, but on it was written 'England'. She opened it carefully and took out a collection of large, black and white pictures: a girl in a church, looking at a tombstone; a girl with straight dark hair, a pointed chin and very pale skin. A Japanese girl. Then a picture of an African man, sitting on a wall in front of a big old house. There was a sign on the wall. Oak Road. She looked carefully at the man. Who did he remind her of?

Then a small colour photograph dropped out onto the floor, face down. There was writing on the back. She picked it up and read it. Chamberlain Square,

Birmingham, April 2000. Fifty years ago. She turned it over. The African man and Japanese girl were standing together in a big square. Joyce looked closer, and then she was sure. It was her grandfather, not grey, heavy and lined as she remembered him but young and slim. He had a camera in one hand and he was wearing a red jacket. His arm was round the dark-haired young Japanese woman and their faces were shining with happiness.

Joyce looked back in the box. In the bottom there was one more black and white photograph. Joyce picked it up. It was the Japanese girl, but this time she was wearing summer clothes and sitting on a bench outside a house. Was the girl looking older? It was hard to tell. The pointed chin and dark eyes were the same, but in this picture her eyes were not laughing. For a moment Joyce felt as though they were looking at her. The girl was sitting on a wooden bench which looked almost new. On the ground in front of her there was a suitcase.

Joyce turned to look at the bench she sat on. It was the same bench that the girl in the photograph was sitting on. The window behind it was the window of her grandfather's house. So the Japanese girl had been here. And her grandfather had been to England. He'd never told her about any journey to England or any visitor from Japan. She wondered who the girl was, how they'd met and why they'd parted. She wondered if she'd ever know the full story.

She sat there for a time in the sun. Then she picked up her video-disk and pressed a button. She spoke softly. 'Hi. I'm in Mungwi. I'm just outside grandfather's house.' In the screen she saw a man's face, young, with dark hair falling over his eyes and a pointed chin. His eyes looked out of the screen from the other side of the world. She continued speaking. 'I've got something to show you...but not on the video-disk. I'd like you to come here, Taka.'

'I've got something to show you too, Joyce,' he said. 'Something you have to read. And I'm already on the plane. I'm coming.'

Joyce put the photos back in the box. She'd look at the rest later. She sat and looked around her. There was a lot of work to be done on the house. It was a crazy place for them to make their home, a thousand kilometres from the sea. But a place where perhaps something had ended too soon. A place where something else could begin.

# After reading

# 读后活动

Choose some of these activities.

1. Hiroshi said: 'You can never really understand someone from another culture.' (page 8) Do you agree?

2. Bernard said: 'I couldn't live all my life in Birmingham, even though I loved it.' (page 61) Do you think you could spend your life in another country?

3. Compare Joyce's life before and after she met Taka. How did she change?

4. What did you enjoy or dislike in *Staying Together*? Write a letter to the author, Judith Wilson, giving your opinions.

5. Write the last page in Ikuko's diary, when she left Zambia to return to Japan.

6. Imagine there is an extra chapter. Write the conversation between Joyce and Taka when they meet again.

7. Make your own activities for other students to do, e.g. match the beginnings and endings.

# Learning guide | 学习指导

## Chapter 1

### New words 生词

- chin /tʃɪn/ *n.* 下巴
- considerate /kənˈsɪdərət/ *a.* 体贴的
- departure /dɪˈpɑːtʃə/ *n.* 离开，离去
- lounge /laʊndʒ/ *n.*（机场等的）等候室
- optimism /ˈɒptɪmɪzəm/ *n.* 乐观（主义）
- pointed /ˈpɔɪntɪd/ *a.* 尖的

### Phrases & expressions 短语和表达

- ahead of...（时间、空间）在……前面
- arrange for sb. to do sth. 安排某人做某事
- (be) unsure of oneself 不自信
- carry on (with...) 继续（……）
- check sth. in 托运（行李）
- get to do sth. 开始做某事
- later on 随后

### Cultural notes 文化点滴

- Birmingham: 伯明翰，位于英格兰中部，是仅次于伦敦的英国第二大城市，工业革命发源地。它是英国主要制造中心之一，现代冶金和

机器制造工业的创始地，也是英国主要铁路、公路干线和运河网的交会点。

• flat / house: flat，英式英语，指公寓、单元房，即一栋住宅楼内的一套房间（包括起居室、卧室、厨房、盥洗室等），在美式英语中为 apartment。house，指单门独户的、单层或多层的房屋住宅。

## Reading exercises 阅读练习

1. Ikuko or Hiroshi? Match the description to the person.
   a) tall...young, with rather untidy hair
   b) a pale serious face with long straight hair and a pointed chin
2. Ikuko thinks: 'Why did the idea of marrying him seem like a door closing on the future?' (page 7) What does Ikuko want to do before getting married?

# Chapter 2

## New words 生词

• corridor /ˈkɒrɪdɔː(r)/ *n.* 走廊
• hostel /ˈhɒstl/ *n.*（大学）宿舍；青年旅社

## Phrases & expressions 短语和表达

• close to... 几乎……；很可能……
• reception desk 服务台，接待处
• send sth. on 把某物转寄

## Cultural note 文化点滴

- Heathrow Airport: 希思罗机场，位于英国伦敦中心以西 23 千米处，是英国最繁忙的机场，也是欧洲旅客运输量最大的国际机场。

## Reading exercise 阅读练习

Ikuko first wrote in her diary: 'Today I arrived in England. It's very exciting.' (page 17) Later she decides to write the truth. What five reasons does she give for feeling unhappy?

# Chapter 3

## New words 生词

- confident /ˈkɒnfɪdənt/ *a.* 自信的
- crooked /ˈkrʊkɪd/ *a.* 歪的；弯的，扭曲的
- darkroom /ˈdɑːkruːm/ *n.*（冲洗照片的）暗室
- develop /dɪˈveləp/ *v.* 冲洗（胶卷）
- funny /ˈfʌni/ *a.* 奇怪的，难以理解的
- receptionist /rɪˈsepʃənɪst/ *n.* 接待员
- wander /ˈwɒndə(r)/ *v.* 徘徊，闲逛

## Phrases & expressions 短语和表达

- be supposed to do sth. 应该做某事
- catch one's attention 吸引某人的注意
- come alive 生动起来
- come up (to sb.)（为交谈）（朝某人）走来

- have sth. in common with sb. 与某人在某方面有共同之处
- hold out sth.（朝某人）伸出（手或胳膊）
- let go of... 松开……；释放……
- manage to do sth. 努力做成某事
- on one's own 一个人，独自；独立地
- work sth. out 找到答案

## Cultural notes 文化点滴

- cooked breakfast:（英国）煮制的早餐。通常指煎蛋加熏肉、香肠或番茄的早餐，一般还会配烤面包片、茶或咖啡。
- IELTS exam: 雅思考试（国际英语语言测试系统），是为打算在以英语为交流语言的国家和地区留学或就业的人群设置的英语语言水平考试。

## Reading exercise 阅读练习

Who or what do the words in *italics* refer to?

| | | | |
|---|---|---|---|
| Lucretia | students at the hostel | | |
| Birmingham | photography | Mike | Ikuko |

a) 'Well... *it*'s sort of grey.'

b) 'Will I have anything in common with *these people*?'

c) ...*she*'s very lively, and kind, too.

d) *She* thought of her camera lying unused on the desk in her room.

e) '*I*'m the one who started the club.'

f) 'Thanks. *It*'s something I really enjoy doing.'

# Chapter 4

## New words 生词

- cathedral /kəˈθiːdrəl/ *n.* 教区总教堂
- ceremony /ˈserəməni/ *n.* 典礼，仪式
- diploma /dɪˈpləʊmə/ *n.* 文凭课程；毕业文凭
- explore /ɪkˈsplɔː(r)/ *v.* 考察，探索
- gallery /ˈgæləri/ *n.* 美术馆，画廊
- personal /ˈpɜːsənl/ *a.* 个人的，私人的
- scholarship /ˈskɒləʃɪp/ *n.* 奖学金
- spicy /ˈspaɪsi/ *a.* 辛辣的

## Cultural note 文化点滴

- nshima: 恩希玛，又译成“希玛”，赞比亚的主食，由玉米粉制成，用手抓着吃。制作方法是先用开水将磨碎的玉米粉和成粥样，然后划动着加入更多的玉米粉，做成黏稠的糊状物。进食时，先要拿一小团放到手掌里，轧制成一个球形，然后浸渍到配菜里。赞比亚人认为烹饪与食用恩希玛的过程是一门艺术。

## Reading exercises 阅读练习

1. Tick (√) the things Ikuko and Bernard talked about.

   a) work and study ☐
   b) English people ☐
   c) food ☐
   d) family ☐
   e) Hiroshi ☐
   f) the future ☐

2. What do you know about Birmingham now?

# Chapter 5

## New words 生词

- flake /fleɪk/ *n.* 小薄片
- shaky /ˈʃeɪki/ *a.*（因惊吓）颤抖的，摇晃的
- tombstone /ˈtuːmstəʊn/ *n.* 墓碑

## Phrases & expressions 短语和表达

- crash into... 撞到……上
- drive off 驾车离开
- in some ways 在某种程度上
- pull oneself + *ad./prep.* 身体用力移动
- start up... 发动……，开动……
- turn off... 离开……，拐出（某条路）

## Reading exercise 阅读练习

Put the events in the right order.

a) At the hostel, Bernard walked with Ikuko to her room.

b) It began to snow.

c) On the way home, a van crashed into the minibus.

d) Bernard took a photo of Ikuko in a church.

e) Ikuko went on the photography trip with Bernard.

f) Ikuko realised she had lost the ring in the accident.

# Chapter 6

## Phrases & expressions 短语和表达

- can't help it 忍不住
- hold on to... 抓住……，握住……
- put sth. away 收起某物
- ring off 挂断电话

## Reading exercise 阅读练习

True, false or don't know?

a) Bernard already knew about Ikuko's boyfriend.

b) Bernard's wife left him and took the children with her.

c) Hiroshi was very calm when Ikuko told him about Bernard.

d) Being with Bernard is a new, exciting experience for Ikuko.

e) Ikuko has decided to leave Hiroshi.

# Chapter 7

## New words 生词

- essay /ˈeseɪ/ *n.* 短论文；散文
- shiver /ˈʃɪvə(r)/ *v.*（尤指因寒冷或恐惧）颤抖，哆嗦
- wardrobe /ˈwɔːdrəʊb/ *n.* 衣柜

## Reading exercises 阅读练习

1. Ikuko asks herself a lot of questions.

'Was I really stupid? Didn't I mean anything to him? Maybe he's back with his wife. Or with someone else. But why hasn't he told me?' (page 51)

What do you think has happened?

2. 'Maybe it was time to go home.' (page 51) Is Ikuko making the right decision?

# Chapter 8

## New words 生词

- address /əˈdres/ *v.* 在（信封、包裹等）上写姓名和地址
- beneath /bɪˈniːθ/ *prep.* 在……下面
- cherry /ˈtʃeri/ *n.* 樱桃；樱桃树
- readdress /ˌriːəˈdres/ *v.* 更改（邮件上的）姓名和地址

## Phrases & expressions 短语和表达

- address sth. to ... 把某物寄给……
- in a hurry 匆匆地

## Reading exercises 阅读练习

1. Complete the summary.

Bernard wrote that Ikuko's letter had been sent to the wrong ________. Bernard's ________ had died ________ weeks after he arrived home. It was impossible for him to leave the ________ or return to ________. Also, his wife wanted to ________ him. He said that he understood if Ikuko wanted to ________ someone from Japan, but he was ________ her very much and asked her to come to Zambia.

2. Bernard wrote: 'I don't know if this life would ever be possible for you.' (page 54) How do you think Ikuko will find life in Africa?

## Chapter 9

### New words 生词

- eventually /ɪˈventʃuəli/ *ad.* 最终
- heavy /ˈhevi/ *a.* 难消化的

### Phrases & expressions 短语和表达

- go out 灯（或火）熄灭
- wet through 湿透

### Reading exercise 阅读练习

True or false?

a) Beatrice spoke good English.

b) Ikuko loved to eat *nshima*.

c) Bernard's house had no electricity.

d) Ikuko left because she didn't like looking after the children.

e) Ikuko felt that she belonged in Japan.

## Chapter 10

### New words 生词

- Arabic /ˈærəbɪk/ *a.* 阿拉伯的；阿拉伯人的
- crossly /ˈkrɒsli/ *ad.* 生气地

- dive /daɪv/ *n.* 潜水
- Egyptian /iˈdʒɪpʃn/ *a.* 埃及的；埃及人的
- filming /ˈfɪlmɪŋ/ *n.* 拍摄；摄影
- gill /gɪl/ *n.* 鳃
- marine /məˈriːn/ *a.* 海（洋）的
- maritime /ˈmærɪtaɪm/ *a.* 海的；海事的
- presentation /ˌpreznˈteɪʃn/ *n.* 演讲，报告
- scuba /ˈskuːbə/ *n.* 水肺（水下呼吸器）
- supersonic /ˌsuːpəˈsɒnɪk/ *a.* 超声速的

## Phrases & expressions 短语和表达

- be in touch with... 与……有联系
- go off 离开
- look up (from...)（从……）抬眼看
- make one's way off... 迅速逃离……

## Reading exercises 阅读练习

1. Complete the information about Joyce Mutanga.
   a) job: ________
   b) age: ________
   c) place of birth: ________
   d) home town: ________
   e) character: ________
2. Why was Taka cross with Joyce?

# Chapter 11

## New words 生词

- coral /ˈkɒrəl/ *n.* 珊瑚

- drop /drɒp/ *n.* 高处到低处的距离
- flipper /ˈflɪpə(r)/ *n.* 脚蹼

## Phrases & expressions 短语和表达

- cool it〈口〉要冷静，别冲动
- every now and then 不时地，常常
- not bad〈口〉非常好；超出预期

## Reading exercises 阅读练习

1. Match the beginnings and endings.

_________ 1) Sven and Taka thought that

_________ 2) Joyce didn't have time to talk

_________ 3) Taka was angry about Joyce's

_________ 4) Joyce remembered everything about fish

_________ 5) After the presentation, Joyce decided

a) rude behaviour towards him.

b) to go for a swim on her own.

c) but forgot people's names and faces.

d) Joyce's presentation was excellent.

e) to Sven about underwater film.

2. What do you think happened to Joyce?

# Chapter 12

## New words 生词

- count /kaʊnt/ *v.* 有价值，有重要性
- hell /hel/ *int.*〈口〉表示愤怒或惊讶

- hum /hʌm/ *v.* 发出嗡嗡声
- moonlit /ˈmuːnlɪt/ *a.* 月光照耀下的；有月光的
- spine /spaɪn/ *n.*（动植物的）刺

## Phrase & expression 短语和表达

- to one's feet 站起来

## Cultural note 文化点滴

- stonefish: 石鱼，少数几种有毒海生鱼类的统称。石鱼行动迟缓，栖息于海底，生活于岩礁、珊瑚间，以及泥底或河口。它们是动物界的伪装高手，能够像石头一样静静地“潜伏”在海床上，等待猎物主动上门。如果人不小心踩到它们，它们会通过背鳍上的刺将大量毒液注入人体内，引起剧痛，甚至使人丧命。

## Reading exercise 阅读练习

Who ...

a) heard Joyce's screams?
b) took the plane to the beach?
c) carried Joyce out of the water?
d) had stepped on a stonefish?
e) took Joyce to hospital?
f) felt more unhappy than angry?

# Chapter 13

## New words 生词

- restless /ˈrestləs/ *a.* 焦躁不安的；不安宁的
- say /seɪ/ *v.* 表示（信息或指令）

## Reading exercise 阅读练习

Put Joyce's memories in the right order.

a) Leaving her home in Zambia with her mother.

b) A voice that was both soft and angry.

c) Wearing her best dress.

d) An argument between her parents.

e) Getting her new shoes dirty.

f) Her presentation the day before.

# Chapter 14

## New words 生词

- beep /biːp/ *v.* 发出哔哔声
- cover /ˈkʌvə(r)/ *n.* 被子，毯子，床单

## Phrases & expressions 短语和表达

- call (sth.) up 调出（某物）备用
- take (sth.) off（离开工作）休假

## Reading exercises 阅读练习

1. Find adjectives that describe Joyce before and after the accident.
2. Joyce thought about 'the people who had been part of her life there, and what they had meant to her.' (page 88) What do you think Joyce needs in her life now?

# Chapter 15

## New words 生词

- headband /ˈhedbænd/ *n.* 束发带
- rock /rɒk/ *v.* 轻轻摇晃

## Phrases & expressions 短语和表达

- cross sth. out 划掉，删掉（错字）
- face up to... 勇敢地面对……
- leave sb./sth. with sb. 把某人 / 某物留给某人
- taste of... 有……味道

## Reading exercise 阅读练习

'She'd never told anyone so much about herself before.' What did Joyce tell Taka?

Write YES or NO after the sentences.

a) Visiting her mother in the USA. _________
b) Childhood memories of Zambia. _________
c) Her research work on the sea. _________
d) Her grandfather, Bernard Chiluba. _________

e) Her hopes for the future. ________

## Chapter 16

### New words 生词

- close-up /ˈkləʊs ʌp/ *n.* 特写（镜头）
- halfway /ˌhɑːfˈweɪ/ *ad.* 在中途；在中间

### Phrases & expressions 短语和表达

- meet up 见面
- pile up 积累；堆积

### Reading exercises 阅读练习

1. Who said what?

   a) ‘You won’t just disappear? We haven’t talked.’

   b) ‘Your hair’s still too long. Just like your grandfather.’

   c) ‘It went really well... And a good opening presentation by a Zambian researcher.’

   d) ‘She’s gone back... To the house where she lived with her grandfather.’

   e) ‘I’m sorry about Bernard.’

   f) ‘It’s a diary I kept for a few months many years ago, before I married your grandfather.’

2. What do you think will happen in the final chapter?

# Chapter 17

## New words 生词

- lined /laɪnd/ *a.*（皮肤）有皱纹的
- part /pɑːt/ *v.*（使）分开

## Phrase & expression 短语和表达

- remind sb. of... 使某人想起……

## Reading exercise 阅读练习

What does Joyce know about her grandfather and the Japanese woman? Write S (sure) or DK (don't know) after the sentences.

a) Her grandfather had been to England. _________

b) He had met a Japanese girl there. _________

c) How they had met. _________

d) The Japanese girl had been to Mungwi. _________

e) Why she had left him. _________

f) What the girl was called. _________

# Translation
# 参考译文

# 相守

## 第一部分　离别

### 第 1 章　承诺

第6页

“我们真的要在这儿吃吗，阿宏？”郁子在一家昂贵的东京饭店门口停下脚步，看上去犹豫不定。

阿宏一边笑着一边为她打开了门。“当然了。今天是你的生日。一切都安排好了。”

饭店里，大厅几乎满座。衣着考究的人们在一起轻声交谈着。服务生把郁子和阿宏带到他们的桌前，并为他们拿来一瓶葡萄酒。郁子感到有些紧张。这不是他们常来的地方。可是，当她看到阿宏在桌对面冲她微笑，黑色的头发像往常一样垂落至双眼，她感觉好多了。

阿宏举起酒杯。“生日快乐，郁子！”他说，“23 岁是什么感觉？”

她笑了。“我真不敢相信。我仍然觉得像是 16 岁。”

当他们快吃完时，两人陷入沉默，看着对方。一支蜡烛在桌上燃烧着，郁子在阿宏的眼眸中能看到烛光。片刻之后，阿宏把手伸进上衣口袋里，掏出了一个小盒子。

## 第7页

“郁子，”他停顿了一下说道，“郁子，你知道我对你的感觉。我从未遇见过其他像你一样的人。我希望你收下这个。我希望我们能永远在一起。”

他把盒子交给桌对面的郁子。郁子双手颤抖着打开了盒子，里面有一枚戒指。那是一枚款式简单的戒指，是爱她的人为她精心挑选的。但是她心里又在想：“这不是发生在我身上的事。”她好像正在看着电影里的一个人。

她知道她父母喜欢阿宏——阿宏体贴入微，在公司表现出色，并且愿意照顾他们唯一的女儿郁子。她的朋友们也喜欢他——他很和善，而且总是乐于帮助有困难的人。郁子知道自己喜欢跟阿宏在一起，他从未让她感到片刻的不开心。她无法想象自己的生活中没有他会怎样。那么为什么一想到嫁给他，就像是关上了通向未来的大门？

阿宏握住郁子的手。郁子抬头看着他。“阿宏，我真的爱你。但是……如果我们现在结婚，以后我要做什么呢？”

“我会照顾你。你不用再工作了。你会有时间做你想做的任何事情。”阿宏的话带着一如既往的乐观。“你可以继续上你的英语课，做更多你喜欢的事情……比如摄影。我们可以买一套公寓——或许有一天甚至可以买一幢带花园的房子，孩子们可以在花园里玩儿。”

## 第8页

“听上去很美好，”郁子回答，“但是我比你年纪小。我还从未真正做过什么事情。我大学毕业后就直接进入了早川公司。你已经经历了许多事——你在美国旅行、留学。你已经见识过这个世界了。”

“郁子，人们把旅行说得非常美好，但是我发现我最喜欢的地方还是日本。我有过美国朋友，的确，但我们从来没有走得很近。你永远无法真正理解一个来自其他文化的人。相信我，最美的地方和最重要的人都在你自己的国家，在你的家乡。”

郁子曾经想过她和阿宏在一起会很快乐。她设想过和他共度人生——只是没这么快。她知道自己必须告诉阿宏她的内心感受，但她还没来得及找出恰当的表达，阿宏就为她找到了。

## 第10页

“郁子，我记得自己曾经有多么渴望旅行。如果那是你真正想做的，我不想让你错失机会。所以如果你想去美国或英国学习几个月，我可以等你。”

“他是如此善解人意。”郁子想。突然间，一切似乎明朗了。

“是的，”她最后说，“我想我需要几个月的时间一个人去看看世界，去多成长一些。你会等我吗？然后我会回来，我们结婚。”

“别成长得太多，郁子。我喜欢你现在的样子。”阿宏说。他温柔地把那枚戒指戴到她的手指上。

* * *

两个月后，在早川大楼的那间大办公室里，郁子最后一次关上了她的电脑。大楼外，东京的天空一片漆黑，高高的写字楼里已经亮起灯光。她从办公桌前站起身来，穿过房间，经过了办公室经理本间老先生的办公桌。她走过的时候，他抬起了头。“好吧，郁子，那么再见了。我们会想你的。对了，你打算去英国哪里？伦敦？”

## 第11页

“不是——是一个叫伯明翰的地方。”郁子回答。

“没听说过。那里美吗？”他问。

“我不知道，不过我会拍很多照片回来的。”

她去拿她的上衣。那是寒冷的十二月里的一天，她站在镜子前戴上了一顶暖和的帽子。她打量着自己。这个从镜子中看向她的女孩儿看起来和两年多前刚开始在那里工作的那个女孩儿没有太大不同：一张白皙严肃的脸庞配着一头长直发和一个尖下巴。她想知道未来的一年会如何改变她——去英国生活，然后是办婚礼。

在乘火车回家的途中，郁子坐在车上回想过去的两年。她很幸运，在早川公司找到了工作。说幸运是因为那是一家很好的公司，并且她发现工作很有乐趣。幸运还因为她在那里遇到了阿宏。

她记得他们相识的那一天。那是一个周五的下午，她在那儿上班只有短短几周，还感觉不太自信。她正在电脑上输入一个销售项目的数据，但是数据结果看上去不对。她深吸了一口气，朝本间先生的办公桌走去，向他报告。本间先生没能帮上什么忙，但他安排了一个程序员来给看一看。

## 第12页

半小时之后，郁子抬起头看见一个头发极其蓬乱的高个子小伙子正穿过房间向她走来。他停下来介绍自己。

“我是增田宏。我听说你的销售项目出了些问题。”他说道。

郁子解释着，阿宏仔细聆听，然后坐下来在电脑上操作起来。突然，他停下，撩起眼前的头发，抬起头看她。他很兴奋。“你绝对正确。程序里有个错误。我知道我们得到的数据有些问题，现在我们可以更改过来了。谢谢！”他站起身来。“好了，你大概该下班回家了吧。你住得远吗？”

“在青梅。坐火车一个小时。”郁子说。

“哦，对，我知道。事实上，我回家会路过青梅，那么我们一直在乘坐同一趟火车。我很惊讶以前我们没见过彼此。”

“嗯，火车太挤了。”郁子说。

“是啊，”他说，“但是我会注意到你的，即使是在人群里。”

那就是故事的开始。此时坐在火车上，在两年以后，郁子记起了他们友谊开始的那些日子：在小餐馆里吃饭，在公园里漫步——慢慢地开始了解彼此。他们发现他们俩曾在同一所初中上学，尽管阿宏比郁子高四届。大学毕业后，他去美国学习计算机课程。他学业优异，但不喜欢美国的生活，于是转而决定返回东京。

## 第13页

在恋爱最初的那段日子，郁子和阿宏一起度过了几乎所有的空闲时光。郁子喜欢他的温柔和善解人意。那是一段完美的爱情，没有争吵，没有令人不快的意外。那难道不是她想要的吗？

“青梅站……青梅站。”郁子听到她要下车的那个站名，突然从思绪中醒来。她下了车，走出拥挤的火车站。在回家的路上，她在一家百货商场门前停了下来——她还需要为这次旅行买一个旅行箱。在走向箱包部时，她经过了一个摆着日记本的架子。她停了下来。那不是她来这儿要买的东西。她多看了一会儿那些日记本，然后选择了一个纯白色封皮的。

在箱包部，她很快选好了要买的箱子。

## 第14页

“我要买那个旅行箱。”她指着一个蓝色的旅行箱说。这个箱子很贵，但她的旅程很长，而且在随后的蜜月旅行，她也可以用到。

* * *

几天后，郁子和阿宏一起坐在成田国际机场里。那只蓝色旅行箱已经被托运上飞往伦敦的航班，而他们正在一起喝最后一杯咖啡。

在来机场的路上他们俩几乎没有说过话。郁子怀疑自己是否在犯一个可怕的错误。“只有六个月。”她对阿宏说，她设法像说服他一样说服自己。

“六个月里能发生很多事，”他说，“我不想失去你。记住你答应了要回来。”

郁子看着她的戒指。“我会回来的。”她说。

他们告别，当她向候机大厅走去时，她最后一次回头望去。阿宏依然站在那儿，他的头发垂落在眼前，在机场的人群中他看上去是那么失落与孤寂。

## 第 2 章　蓝色旅行箱

### 第15页

“您能描述一下旅行箱的样子吗？”希思罗机场服务台的女工作人员问。郁子感觉想哭。这是一次糟糕的乘机经历。她坐在两个孩子旁边，他们一直很吵，一刻也坐不住。郁子根本无法入睡。而此刻她的旅行箱又丢了，里面装着她的衣服、相机——所有东西。

她用英语慢慢地说道：“是蓝色的……”

女工作人员亲切地对她微笑着。“别担心，填写一下这个表格就行。我确信我们能找到它。箱子很可能在下一班飞机上，我们会转寄给您。”

郁子缓慢地填写着手提箱的外观和里面装的东西，以及她将暂住的地址：伯明翰市塞利奥克区奥克路塞利园公寓。

漫长的四个小时之后，出租车开到一座被树木环绕的古老的大房子前。现在是七点钟。从希思罗机场到这里是一段漫长而艰辛的旅程——先坐伦敦地铁，然后换乘去伯明翰的火车，最后从火车站乘出租车抵达公寓。

## 第16页

郁子向公寓走去。她觉得这幢建筑就像她见过的图片里那种有深色石墙和尖形窗户的教堂。两名学生从大门走出，用郁子听不懂的语言交谈着。她走了进去。接待处没人，但有一个指示牌，写着“需要服务请按铃”。她按了铃。

片刻之后，一扇门开了，一个女人走了出来。“有什么需要帮忙的吗？”

“我是郁子……金泽郁子。”

“哦，对了。我们正等你呢。你住 31 号房间。跟我来，我带你去。你的旅行箱在哪儿？”

郁子开始跟她讲述，但那个女人似乎并没有在听。

“哦，亲爱的，不要紧，”她说，“好了，这是你的房间。现在晚餐已经结束了，不过如果你想吃东西的话，在离这儿五分钟路程的布里斯托尔路上有很多餐馆。八点吃早餐——在主楼一层后面。好吗？明白了吗？”

“明白了。”郁子说着关上房门，屋里剩下她一个人。可是她不确定自己是不是已经明白了，那个女人说的话听起来跟她在英语课上听过的录音不一样。也许是因为郁子太疲惫了吧。

## 第17页

她环顾房间：一张床、一个写字台、一盏灯。她想洗个澡，但没有毛巾。她不饿，而且她无论如何都无法面对在那个夜晚自己一个人走到又冷又陌生的街道上。她想给阿宏打个电话——但日本现在是凌晨四点。

这个房间有些冷，于是她上床取暖。她很累，但大脑还很兴奋。她从手提包里掏出新日记本，开始用英语写起日记来。

2000年1月9日

今天我抵达英国了。非常兴奋。

她想了一会儿。"我在写给谁呢?"她自忖道，"我会给阿宏看吗?或者就是给我自己的?不管怎样，我应该如实写。"她开始重写。

今天我抵达英国了。我的旅行箱丢了。这段旅途很艰辛。我很沮丧，因为我听不太懂英国人说话。此刻，我正在学生公寓自己的房间里。我感觉很孤独。我想念阿宏。也许他对于旅行的理解是正确的。

## 第18页

她放下笔，感觉快要哭了。这并非她所期待的在英国第一天的感受。她把头枕在枕头上——也许她休息一下就会感觉好点儿……

* * *

一阵敲门声还有一个男人的声音传来。"金泽郁子吗?"

房间昏暗，郁子一时不知身在何处。她打开灯，看了看手表。是周一早上七点，她在英国。

敲门声又响起，接着是远去的脚步声。郁子从床上起来，然后意识到自己还穿着全套衣服。她感觉又热又不舒服。

她走到门前把门打开。一个男人的身影正消失在走廊尽头。她只看到了他的背影——黑头发，红夹克。而门前放着她的蓝色旅行箱。

## 第3章　第一个星期

### 第19页

郁子把旅行箱提进屋里，她感觉好多了。现在她可以冲个澡，然后换身衣服。但是她必须先给阿宏打个电话。她从手提包里拿出手机拨通他的号码。

“那么伯明翰什么样儿？”他问道，声音听起来十分遥远。他永远理解不了为什么郁子想去伯明翰学习，而不是去牛津或剑桥这类更知名的地方。但是她不想待在旅游中心，即使那里很漂亮。她想看看英国人真正的生活是怎样的。

但是现在她不那么确定了。她走到狭小卧室的窗前向外看。外面有一条狭窄的马路，路边停着汽车，还种着几棵光秃秃的树。在晨曦中，一切看起来寒冷而暗淡。

“嗯，”她说道，“是某种灰暗的感觉。”

一小时后，郁子找到了公寓的餐厅。她羞怯地走了进去。里面弥漫着油炸食品的味道，还有人们小声交谈的声音。她环顾周围，虽然有些是几个人坐在一起，但是也有不少是一个人。“也许我不是唯一一个新生。”她想。

## 第20页

一个身材高大的女人走过来说："亲爱的，你是新来的吗？你想要一份熟食早餐吗？"

郁子一脸困惑。熟食早餐是什么？但那个女人变得不耐烦了。"培根加鸡蛋？"她大声问。

"好……好的，谢谢。"郁子回答道。

郁子独自坐在那儿吃饭的时候，很想知道餐厅里有没有英国学生。她看到一群日本学生——一个一头亮黄色头发戴耳环的男生和两个穿着紧身时尚服装的女生。离她更近的是一群用英语和另一种语言交谈的女生。每个人看上去都很年轻。

"我和这些人会有共同之处吗？"她想，"也许我就应该搭个航班回日本去。"

她深吸了一口气。她已经拿到了自己的旅行箱，事情还不算太糟。该去上英语课了，她吃完早饭走出了餐厅。

## 第21页

十分钟后她走到街上。她拿出发给她的标有去语言中心路线的地图开始走。她应该坐公交车，但是公交站在哪儿呢？她努力在地图上找。

这时有人用日语跟她说话："你要去语言中心吗？"

她转过身，是那个黄头发的日本男生。他和另外两个学生在一起，一个黑头发的女生和一个比他还高的男生。

"是……是的，"她对那个日本男生说，"坐65路公交车吗？"

"对，"接着他继续用英语说道，"跟我们一起走吧，我们也去那儿。"

那天晚上她坐在酒吧里，面前是一杯喝了一整晚的温啤酒，郁子意识到自己已经有朋友了。坐在她对面的是那个黄头发的日本男生，他的名字叫俊井。“大家叫我疯子俊井。”他大笑着说。他来英国很久了，而且看起来认识所有人。坐在他旁边的是来自意大利的彼得罗，坐在郁子旁边的是柳克丽霞，就是早晨和俊井在一起的那个黑头发女生。她来自南美洲，在巴西一个叫累西腓的城市。在教室时，柳克丽霞已经指给她看过这座城市在地图上的位置。

## 第22页

郁子喜欢柳克丽霞温暖的笑容，还有她碧绿的眼睛和那自信的英语。她说话快到郁子很难跟得上。

“哦，是的，”他们坐在酒吧里聊天时柳克丽霞说，“但我的写作一点儿也不好！我必须得提高。”

“你来这儿多久了？”郁子问。

“三个月。我需要通过雅思考试，接着我就可以去念大学的商科。”

随后，他们所有人一起穿过漆黑的街道走回了公寓。

“谁想来点儿上好的意大利咖啡？”彼得罗问，但是突然间郁子只想一个人待会儿。她和其他人道了晚安，回到自己的房间，但在睡觉前她拿出了日记本。

2000 年 1 月 10 日

真是漫长的一天啊……发生了这么多事情。我的旅行箱到了。我去上了我的第一堂英语课，还结交了一些来自不同国家的朋友。一整天都用英语讲话非常难。大家都很友好，但他们年龄都比我小一点儿。我喜欢柳克丽霞，她很活泼，也很亲切。我们去了酒吧。很难听懂大家说的话，那里很吵。不过，大家看起来玩儿得都很开心。但这并不完全是我所期待的。我究竟在期待什么呢？我不知道。

第23页

* * *

周五下午郁子坐在咖啡馆里等柳克丽霞时，她不敢相信自己到英国才五天，感觉上要更久。她在公寓已经感觉像在家一样自在，她开始熟悉自己所在的伯明翰这个小角落那些树木成行的街道。

她漫步走到咖啡馆墙上的布告栏前。在许多迪斯科舞会和电影的布告中有一则引起了她的注意。

摄影俱乐部

下次聚会：1 月 15 日周六下午 2 点，261 室

人物摄影——伯纳德·奇卢巴

欢迎参加

她想起了闲置在房间书桌上的相机。上初中时，她曾是摄影俱乐部的成员。再多学点儿摄影知识是件好事——而且还能拍些照片给阿宏看。周六下午，就在明天。她记下了地点和时间。

第24页

就在这时，柳克丽霞来到她身后。“哦，摄影。这应该是个很不错的俱乐部。可是周六是购物的日子，难道你不想进城转转吗？”

“谢谢，但是我不怎么喜欢购物。”郁子回答道。

“不喜欢？”柳克丽霞一脸惊讶地说，“真奇怪，我超爱购物。好吧，五点左右到我房间来，我要给你展示一下我的购物成果。”

* * *

第二天下午两点，郁子羞怯地打开了 261 室的房门。那是个小房间，里面挤满了正在交谈的人。那儿的人她谁都不认识，但一个留着棕色卷发、戴眼镜的年轻人向她走过来。

“嗨，欢迎。你是来参加俱乐部的吗？”

“对……我想是的。”郁子说。

“太好了。我叫迈克，是这个俱乐部的创始人。那么你叫……？”

“郁子。你们在这个俱乐部做些什么？”

“嗯，这其实就是提供了一个聚会并互相帮助的机会，”迈克解释道，“我们有一间暗室，所以如果你想的话可以在这里冲洗照片……”

## 第25页

“冲洗？”郁子没有听懂。

“是的，你不用把胶卷拿到照相馆，你可以学习自己洗照片——尽管洗出来只是黑白的，不是彩色的。另外我们会一起出去拍照片。通常就在伯明翰拍，但有时我们会去乡下。”

他说话很快，但郁子努力听懂了。她很高兴。除了她的老师们，她还没有和很多英国人真正地说过话。

“你之前摄影经验多吗？在……日本，对吧？”迈克问。

“只有一点儿。但我想多学点儿。”郁子回答。

“好，今天伯纳德要给我们展示一些照片，是他在伯明翰拍摄的人物照。伯纳德·奇卢巴，在那边。”迈克指向一个背对着他们站着的高个子男生——他留着很短的黑色卷发，穿着红色夹克。她以前在哪里见过这件红夹克呢？

听到自己的名字，那个男生转身向他们走过来。他的皮肤是深棕色，几乎是黑色，光滑油亮。他看起来比其他学生年龄要大一点儿。

“伯纳德，这是郁子。”迈克说。

## 第26页

伯纳德露出一个大大的笑容，在他黝黑的脸上牙齿显得格外白。郁子注意到他笑的时候脸有些歪，一边咧得比另一边大。他伸出手，郁子看着他握了上去。

“你好，郁子。”

他有力地握住她的手。他的声音低沉，郁子喜欢他柔缓地念出自己的名字。他继续说：“不过我想我们是邻居。你是有个蓝色旅行箱的郁子吗？”

这时郁子想起第一天早晨看见的在走廊尽头消失的红夹克。

她松开了他的手，突然一阵害羞。“哦……谢谢你……是的，是我的旅行箱。你怎么……怎么知道箱子是我的？”

“箱子从机场送来的时候我正要离开公寓。当时是清晨，接待员很忙——所以我就说我给她拿上去吧。”

“哦，谢谢……你真是太好了。”她注意到他说话特别清楚。他的语速不太快，不像她遇到的其他所有人那样，也不急于在她回应前继续讲话。

“那么你来自日本？”他问。

“是的……你呢？”

## 第28页

“我来自赞比亚，在非洲。”

大家开始在他们周围就座。“好了，失陪了，郁子。”迈克说完，走到前面为伯纳德开场。郁子听伯纳德用低沉的声音讲解着照片，她之前从没有见过像那样的照片。所有的照片都是他在伯明翰拍的，但是照片中的人好像来自世界各地：牙买加、巴基斯坦、中国。郁子怀疑自己能否学会让静止不动的面孔变得那般生动。

活动结束时，她走向伯纳德。“谢谢。这些照片真的太精彩了。”

伯纳德对她笑了笑。“谢谢。这是我真正喜欢做的事情。”他有点儿不确定地看着她。“我们正要去喝咖啡。你想来吗？”

郁子看了看手表，四点半了。她想起她要回公寓和柳克丽霞见面。“不了……对不起，我去不了。我跟人有约了。”

“哦，好吧。”他说完转身走了。

## 第 4 章　市中心

### 第29页

接下来的星期六，郁子醒得很早。她向窗外望去，几乎是第一次看到了太阳，阳光照耀在隔壁花园的树上。多美的早晨啊！“一整天没事，”她想，“我真的应该更勇敢一点儿。我还没有真正地逛过伯明翰。”她决定去探索一番。

一小时过后，她在等公交车了。车来了，她买了一张去市中心的车票，并坐在了靠近前部的一个空位上。车门关上了，但是一阵奔跑的脚步声传来，车门再次打开，让一个人上了车。郁子看到一件红夹克，并且听出了对司机讲话的那个深沉的声音。“谢谢。去市中心。”

他几乎快要从郁子身旁走过去了，突然她听到自己说：“伯纳德？”

他惊讶地抬起头。“哦，郁子。我没看见你。”他边说边坐在了她旁边。在狭窄的公交车座位上她感觉到他离得很近。两人沉默了片刻，接着他们同时开口说话。

### 第30页

“你是……”

“我没见到你……”

他们大笑起来。“继续说。”伯纳德说。

“我没见到你……你还住在公寓里吗?”

“当然，但是我比大多数人起得早。我通常第一个去吃早餐。”

“你不在语言中心学习，是吗?”

“是的，我在教育系。我在攻读教学方向的文凭，所以我一天中的大部分时间都在大学里度过——而且晚上我也在学校里吃饭。”

“你的课程难吗?”她问他。

“难，有很多功课，但是我已经习惯繁重的课业了。我在家乡已经是一名教师了，但我获得了政府奖学金，资助我到这里求学拿文凭。”

她想知道他在赞比亚的生活是什么样子。“你住在首都吗?”她问。

“不。我来自赞比亚北部，一个叫芒戈的小镇。那里只有一所学校和几家商店。我们甚至连一家医院也没有。根本没有高大的建筑。不像伯明翰。”他微笑着说，并露出了她之前注意过的有些歪的笑容。“那今天上午你打算在伯明翰做什么？你要去购物吗?”

## 第31页

“不，”郁子回答，“我只想在伯明翰转转。”

“这是个不错的城市，我喜欢它，”他说，“很多人对这个城市有抱怨。但它是充满活力的。它一直在成长，一直在变化。”

此刻，在他们四周，高大的建筑在阳光下熠熠生辉。接着公交车驶入一条狭窄的街道，停了下来。

“我们该下车了。”他们跟着其他乘客下了车。然后伯纳德转向她。“如果你愿意……我可以带你稍微转转伯明翰。”

“好啊，谢谢，”郁子说，“我非常愿意。”

他们一起穿过伯明翰市中心，走进星期六熙熙攘攘的人群中。伯纳德带她逛了绿色小花园中的小教堂、美术馆，以及在一些工厂旧址上建起的新的商店和餐馆。他们谈论着眼前的景色，谈论伯明翰，谈论自己的国家。郁子几乎没有注意到自己疲惫的双脚和寒风。

这时伯纳德看了看自己的手表。“到午饭时间了，已经一点多了。你想做什么？”

## 第32页

“我们去餐馆怎么样？”她提议道，“或者我们可以回公寓去？”

“我没法面对公寓的饭，”伯纳德说，“咱们去一家印度餐馆吧。我知道这附近有一家很好。”

餐馆很小，但是温暖又亲切。印度服务员见到他们很高兴。“嗨，伯纳德。你还好吗？你的相机在哪儿？”

“你之前见过他，”伯纳德对郁子说，“在那些照片里。”他教她如何用手指把面包片和辣肉一起夹着吃。“这是我们在家乡的吃法。我们不用刀叉，这样食物吃起来才更好吃。但在赞比亚我们主要吃恩希玛，不吃面包和土豆。哦，我想念恩希玛！”

“是的，我想念米饭。公寓里也有米饭，但和日本的米饭不一样，太硬了。”郁子说。

“那在日本你们用木棍吃饭，是吗？”

“筷子？是的，很容易。我来教你！但我们不是一直用筷子——有时我们用吃西餐的方式吃饭。”

“你和家人一起住吗？”他问。这是他问她的第一个私人问题。

“是的。”她不知道该不该告诉他关于阿宏的事，但现在似乎不是恰当的时候。伯纳德也沉默了片刻，郁子想他是不是想家了。“你呢?”她问,“你和父母一起住吗?”

## 第33页

“不,我父母年纪很大。他们自己住……”他看起来好像欲言又止。

郁子感觉这不是他想聊的事情。她等了一会儿,然后换了话题。“你拍照多久了?”

“哦,很长时间了。这一直是我的爱好。不过我正着手创业,做照相生意。”他说。

“在教学之外?”郁子问。

“是的。这会是一项艰巨的工作,但是我可以做好。人们总是想拍照片。他们需要护照照片,还有其他证件照,在一些特殊时刻也需要拍照——婚礼和其他庆典。芒戈没有摄影师,所以如果我能自己冲洗照片,意味着我能赚更多钱。你呢,郁子?你在日本有工作吗?”

“没有,再没有了,”她说,“我辞职了。”

“那么你回到日本会做什么?”

郁子看着她手指上的戒指。“我不太清楚,”她说,“有人……”

## 第34页

“我明白了,”伯纳德说,“我懂。”

2000 年 1 月 22 日

今天我和伯纳德一起在伯明翰度过了一个上午。他带我看了很多东西。今晚他还邀请我去见他的朋友。我们要去听赞比亚音乐,品尝赞比亚美食。我希望我们可以成为好朋友。他和我在这里认识的其他人都不一样,和我认识的任何人都不一样。

# 第 5 章　下雪

## 第35页

“那么这个周末你又要和伯纳德一起出去?”星期六的早晨，柳克丽霞正坐在郁子的房间里喝着咖啡。她的视线越过咖啡杯望向郁子。

“是参加摄影俱乐部。我们要去乡下，去一个叫宽街的地方。”郁子回答说。

柳克丽霞扬起眉毛，什么也没说。郁子知道她在想什么。

“我们只是朋友，柳克丽霞。真的。他知道我在日本有人了。”

“可是，郁子，日本的那个人知道伯纳德吗?”柳克丽霞问。

“不是你想的那样，”郁子开始说，“我和伯纳德……在某些方面我们很像。我们喜好相同，但是我们不谈论他和我之间那类的事情。”她看了看自己的戒指。“我还什么都没有跟阿宏说。我不想让他担心……为了不存在的事。”

“但是真的什么都没有吗?”柳克丽霞问，“因为有时我看到你们两个在一起，看起来好像有些什么。”

## 第36页

“不，没有更多的了。我们去散步。我们很聊得来。我了解了很多不同的地方和人……关于非洲的、赞比亚的，包括那儿的故事、那儿的音乐。我在学习跳舞。”郁子想起跳舞时和伯纳德手牵手的感觉。

当郁子和伯纳德在一起时，似乎一切都很美好。那么为什么她感觉这么困惑?

“小心点儿，郁子。”

“我没事的，柳克丽霞，真的。”

* * *

“好的，所有人，出发！”迈克发动了小巴车，然后驱车穿过灰色的街道，接着沿着高速公路行驶，开进乡村。郁子和伯纳德看向窗外冰封的旷野和阴云密布的天空。郁子意识到自己在来回转手指上的戒指，伯纳德也异乎寻常地沉默。他们驶离了高速公路，随着道路变得越来越窄，山势愈发陡峭，车子慢下来。很快他们来到了一个村庄，小巴车停在了街边。

“好了，各位，我们到了，”迈克走过来打开侧车门时说，“我希望你们都穿了保暖的衣服——冷极了！我建议咱们在村子里转转，在天黑前拍些照片，然后四点钟回这里的茶社集合。”

## 第37页

下车时寒风向众人袭来。他们正在一条街的中央，两边是古老的小房子。尽管才两点钟，但是家家户户都亮起了灯。他们缩着脑袋，顶着寒冷一起向前走。队伍里一些人停下来走进了小商店，但是迈克、郁子和伯纳德继续走，直到走到一座古老的教堂前。他们顺着小路向教堂门口走去。小路的两边是灰色的墓碑，上面刻着几百年前去世并被埋葬于此的人的名字。墓碑间开满了小白花。

“这些花叫什么？”郁子问。

“它们是雪花莲——春天开得最早的花。”迈克说。

郁子拿着她的相机弯下身，试图给小花拍照，但是天太黑了。几片雪花飘落下来。

“雪，”伯纳德说，“这么说雪就是这样的。我以前从没见过。”他微笑着转向郁子。

“咱们去教堂里面吧。”迈克说。

里面有石头和蜡烛的气味。他们静静地走着。

## 第38页

“郁子，看。”伯纳德指向一块古老的墓碑。上面有一个女人的石像，双手交叉躺着。郁子看着它，好奇这个女人有着怎样的一生。她看着很年轻——和郁子年龄相仿。突然，一道闪光照亮了黑暗，郁子惊讶地抬起头。伯纳德拿着他的相机站在那儿。“你站在那里看起来很美，就像是石头雕刻的。”他说。

他们从教堂里出来时，雪下得更大了，地已经白了。

“咱们争取拍些照片。”伯纳德说。

但是迈克很担心。“我不喜欢拍这个，”他说，“咱们最好回去。”他们匆匆忙忙回到茶社，发现其他人已经在那里了。郁子想待一会儿暖和暖和，但是已经没有时间了。

“对不起，”迈克说，“但是上高速之前这段路况很差。咱们得尽快离开。”

他们回到了小巴车里。郁子和伯纳德坐在靠前的座位，伯纳德靠窗。迈克坐上驾驶座然后出发了，他开得很慢，很小心。大家都很安静。小巴车开始上山，速度非常缓慢。

突然他们前方出现灯光，接着一阵撞击好像径直穿过了郁子的身体。她听到尖叫声，感觉自己被抛向前窗。有玻璃碎裂的声音。

## 第39页

一秒钟后，郁子横躺在小巴车座位上，几乎躺到了地上。伯纳德的双臂紧紧地抱着她。

“伯纳德……？”

“嗯……你还好吗？”

“我想还好。”她小心地艰难起身。车厢后面的人正在喊叫，但是车厢前面一切都很安静。她站起来向着驾驶位挪动。发动机还在运转，但是迈克不动了。他脸朝下趴在座位上，头发上全是玻璃碴儿，湿润的雪花透过破碎的窗户吹进来。

郁子伸手关掉了发动机。现在她能听到外边的声音了。另一辆车，一辆小货车的司机已经从车里下来了，正和其他学生说话。雪色朦胧中她只能看见他们。

她朝迈克俯下身，轻轻地抬起他的脸，眼前的景象让她感到害怕。伯纳德来到她身后，她朝他转过身。“他还有呼吸，”她说，“我们要为他寻求救助。我的手机……在我的包里——很可能在地上什么地方。你能找到吗？”

## 第40页

过了一会儿，伯纳德拿着手机回来了，但是她意识到自己不知道应该拨什么号码，向谁寻求帮助或者说什么。她把电话给了伯纳德。外面的人一直在说话。突然间似乎只能等待，别无他法，雪继续下着。

那天深夜，他们俩一起回到了公寓。两个人都很沉默。伯纳德陪郁子走到她的房间。他们站在门外，她找着钥匙。接着片刻间，他们彼此对视。她想起那辆小货车撞向他们时他是如何抱着她的。“谢谢你，伯纳德。”她说道。

“你现在没事了吧？”他问。

“是的，”郁子说，“没事了，谢谢。”她走进房间。她听着伯纳德走开的脚步声，然后在床上坐了一会儿。“也许我应该给阿宏打个电话。”她想。这时她想起伯纳德还拿着她的手机。

她决定泡个澡，于是在热水里躺了很长时间。直到穿好衣服，她才意识到有东西丢了。那枚戒指不在她的手指上了。“也许撞车时我把它弄丢了。”她想。但是那似乎并不重要。

### 第41页

她坐在房间里，回想这一天，不知道迈克怎么样了。她仍然感觉摇摇晃晃。这时外面传来脚步声和敲门声。她打开门。伯纳德拿着她的手机站在那里。他把手机还给了她。“我给医院打电话询问了迈克的情况。他们说他现在清醒了，而且看起来不错。他必须要在医院待些日子，但是他会好起来的。”

突然，郁子觉得承受不住了。她从门口转身离开，开始哭泣。接着她感到伯纳德的双臂抱住了她。“郁子，没事。一切都会好起来。”他们就那样待了许久，直到她不再哭泣。她意识到自己想要这样，紧挨着他。

## 第 6 章　坦白

### 第42页

明媚的阳光透过郁子卧室薄薄的窗帘照进来。那是星期日的早晨。一阵敲门声传来，是柳克丽霞的声音：“你还好吗？我们都听说了发生的事。我给你带些早餐来好吗？”

“哦，我没事。我很好。不过我不想吃早餐，谢谢。”郁子没有开门。

她转向伯纳德，柔声说道：“我必须和你谈谈……有些事我得告诉你。”

“我也是……我也有很多事要告诉你。不过我们有时间。”

郁子下床拉开窗帘。阳光洒满了房间。外面的街道被雪覆盖，白茫茫一片。天空蔚蓝，阳光明媚。“来吧，”伯纳德说，“咱们去走走，这样可以聊聊。”

在雪地里行走很困难。郁子紧紧抓住伯纳德的胳膊。空气很冷，但是风已经停了。周围很安静。只有几辆车缓慢地沿着道路行驶，在雪地上留下黑色的车辙。

## 第43页

“伯纳德……我不知道自己是怎么了。我在日本已经有男朋友了。”

“是的，我知道。你想跟我说说他的事吗？”

“他叫阿宏。我们在一起两年了。他是我第一个真正的男朋友。我们计划今年晚些时候结婚。但我想先去旅行，看看新的地方。他毫不介意。他信任我……”

“你告诉他什么了吗？”伯纳德问。

“没有，”她答道，“我想也许没有什么可告诉的。直到昨晚。”

“郁子，我也有些事情必须告诉你。”伯纳德停下来，从他的钱包里拿出一张小照片。他把它递给郁子。两个眼睛溜圆、表情严肃的非洲孩子在照片中凝视着。郁子看看照片，然后看看伯纳德。她什么也没说。

过了一会儿，伯纳德说：“这是比阿特丽斯，十一岁了。查尔丽五岁。”他指着两个女孩儿分别说道。

终于，郁子找到了合适的话语。“那你结婚了？”

“我十二年前就结婚了。我那时很年轻。我们俩都很年轻，太年轻了。”

“那么发生了什么？”郁子问。

## 第44页

“她离开了我。她回到了卢萨卡，回到了首都，她的家人在那里生活。她离开了我和孩子们。”

“那么……孩子们怎么样了？”

“我一个人把她们养大，”伯纳德回答，“很不容易。最初是我的母亲帮我，但她现在年纪大了。所以当我得到来英国学习的机会时，我就让我的妻子在我不在的时候回到芒戈来照顾孩子们，就一年。”

他们在那里站了一会儿。郁子想问伯纳德为什么以前不告诉她。但是她没有问。她把照片还给了他。

“她们很可爱，可爱的孩子们。”她说。

“是的，”他边把照片收好边说，“我很想念她们。”他们又开始走，肩并肩，但是没有接触。

“也许我们不该再见面了。”郁子说。她低头看着自己站在雪中的双脚，雪已经融化成了脏兮兮的灰色雪水。

“昨晚的事我很抱歉。”伯纳德说。

郁子突然感觉很愤怒。“真的吗？你真的感到抱歉吗？”

“不是，郁子。我很抱歉之前我没有向你解释。如果你不想再看到我，我会理解。但是我并不后悔昨晚发生的事。”

## 第46页

郁子想想过去的几周。然后她停下来看着他。“不，我也不后悔昨晚的事，”她说，“而且我还想再见到你。”

那天深夜，郁子拿着手机独自坐在她的房间里。她深吸一口气，按下了记忆键。那是阿宏的号码。

这时是日本的早晨，阿宏刚刚起床。这场谈话并不容易。她先和他说了那场事故。

“我几乎从座位上被抛了出去，但是坐在我旁边的人，伯纳德，他救了我。”

“伯纳德？他是英国人吗？”阿宏立刻问道。

她已经忘了阿宏有多了解她，已经忘了一旦她有什么大事，阿宏马上就能感觉到。

“不，他是赞比亚人。”郁子回答。

“什么？”阿宏说。

“来自非洲。”

“那他是你的男朋友？告诉我。”

“是，”郁子慢吞吞地说道，“是的，我想是的。我真的不知道将来会怎样。我非常抱歉，阿宏。”

她从来没见过阿宏生气，但是她知道此刻他很愤怒。“你承诺过的，我等你了，”他大喊道，“但是我知道出事了，我知道你不一样了。我现在该怎么办？”

## 第47页

“哦，阿宏。对不起，对不起。”但是他已经挂了电话。

她在那儿坐了一会儿，无所适从。然后她拿出日记本。也许她把所有的事情都写下来，能觉得更清晰一点儿。她拿出笔开始写。一小时后她仍然在写。

我不知道自己对伯纳德是什么感觉，但是自从遇见他就感觉好像有一扇门打开了——有很多新想法、新体验。我们在一起是如此开心。我对阿宏感觉很愧疚，但是我没办法。我想我是爱过他的。我相信他，他也相信我。但是他想要的是平静的、安定的生活，在家乡日本生活。我想我无法过那样的生活。无论如何，现在还不行。我不知道将来会发生什么，但是我很高兴我来到了英国。

## 第 7 章　来自赞比亚的消息

### 第48页

那是三月末一个有风的星期日下午。伯纳德和郁子正坐在伯纳德的房间里。郁子在看一份英文报纸，不时停下来翻翻词典查单词。伯纳德在写文章，满地都是书和写满字的纸。CD 传出的音乐在房间里回荡，穿过敞开的窗户飘到春天的空气里。

日本似乎离这个充满非洲音乐的房间很远。郁子给阿宏写过信，试图对发生的事做出更多的解释。过了一段时间，她收到了他的回信。

我仍然想你，并且希望你不会受到伤害。我希望你能回日本，这样我们能好好谈一谈。但最终你必须决定你想要什么。

敲门声响起。“请进。”伯纳德喊道。柳克丽霞探头进来。“你好。有你一份传真，伯纳德。之前在前台，我把它带过来了。给你。”她把那张纸递给他，就离开了。

### 第49页

伯纳德看了那手写的寥寥几行字。然后他抬起头，表情严肃。“是比阿特丽斯写的。我的妻子回卢萨卡了。她抛下了比阿特丽斯和查尔丽，留下她们独自生活。”

他默默思考了一会儿，然后继续说：“郁子，我必须回去。她们年纪太小，无法照顾自己。我的父母年纪大了，而且有病在身。没有别人了。”

“你的学业怎么办……还有我们？”郁子问。

“我不知道。但是郁子，这不会是我们的结局。我们一定要再相见，但我不知道怎么做。”

三天后，郁子和伯纳德一起站在希思罗机场。郁子想起她上一次在机场告别的情景——在日本。她那时给阿宏的承诺现在怎么样了？她那时是认真的。她哆嗦了一下，突然觉得很冷。伯纳德搂住了她。

“我一到芒戈，就给你发传真，”他说，“打国际长途的电话不太好用。你有我学校的地址——你可以随时往那里给我写信。记住，郁子，我们很快会再见面的，在某个地方。”郁子最后一次感受伯纳德的拥抱。

## 第50页

“很快会再见的。”她总算说出一句。她注视着他的红色夹克消失远去。

* * *

2000 年 5 月 4 日

伯纳德离开才一个月。还是没有消息，什么都没有。没有信，没有传真，没有电话。我不相信他不在乎我，我不相信他已经把我忘了。我忘不了他。

郁子独自坐在房间里看着窗外。现在树已经绿了，不是嫩绿，看着已经是深绿了。没有什么别的可写。那天她什么特别的事都没有做。去上课了，但是什么也没学到。她知道她的老师和朋友们都担心她。过去的一个月里，她睡不好。她的面庞消瘦，脸色甚至比平时还要白。她给阿宏写了信——一封简短的信，信中告诉他伯纳德回家了，但是除此之外没说别的。

她试过给伯纳德发传真，但是他给她的号码接不通。她寄了一封又一封信，也没有回音。她夜里好几个小时睡不着，翻来覆去地想着同样的问题。“真的是我傻吗？我对他来说什么也不算吗？也许他和他的妻子一起回去了。或者和其他人。但是他为什么不告诉我？”

### 第51页

这时她身旁书桌上的手机响起来。她拿起手机，心跳加速。

“郁子，你好吗？”是阿宏。

“我还好。你好吗？你收到我的信了吗？”

“收到了，”他停顿了一下，“那你现在在做什么？”

“学习……没做什么事。”郁子回答。

“你还是计划待到七月吗？”阿宏问。

“我不知道。我还没想过这件事。”她说。

“郁子，回日本吧。回到这儿来。我会去机场接你。最好还是……”

“也许你是对的。我会考虑的。谢谢，阿宏。”她慢慢地放下手机。和他聊天真好，用自己的语言和认识从前的郁子的人说话真好。也许他是对的，也许是时候回家了。

她打开她的衣柜，拉出蓝色旅行箱。

## 第 8 章　等待

### 第52页

郁子和阿宏在青梅公园的樱花树下漫步。树的花期已过，已经是夏天了。郁子已经回来一个月了，但是她和阿宏彼此间仍然小心翼翼。她知道自己对他伤害很深，也知道他不确定该怎么办。郁子一直没有聊过她对伯纳德的感情，而阿宏也没问过她任何问题。

"你想在这儿歇歇吗？"阿宏问。树下有一个空座位。星期日下午公园里挤满了人。他们旁边坐着一对带宝宝的年轻夫妇。她看到阿宏在看那个婴儿，他的头发像往常一样垂落于眼前。她想他会是一个非常好的父亲。而她不能期待阿宏会一直等她，直到她对自己的感情做出选择。

她甚至不再确定自己的感觉。她仍然不能忘记伯纳德。她几乎不再期待收到他的消息了，但是她又忍不住有些期盼。她把自己的地址留给了公寓，每天早晨她都等着邮件到来。但是既没有来自英国的信，也没有来自赞比亚的信。

## 第53页

第二天早晨，郁子躺在床上挣扎着起床。"但是为什么要起床？"她想。那天她没有什么事情可做，除了找工作——而她知道自己不会去找。

她去给自己冲了杯咖啡，然后坐下来喝着。这时邮件到了。有一封信，一封装在航空信封里的信。信上贴着赞比亚的邮票。一封给她寄往伯明翰而后改寄到日本的信。

她坐着，看着那信封，拿在手里翻来覆去地看。她在想自己期望在信里看到什么。她拆开了信封，开始看。

亲爱的郁子：

我刚刚收到一封你的来信，尽管我想这不是你的第一封信了。这封信花了很长时间才到。他们把信送错了学校，又没有人转寄。学校的传真机坏了。我们正在等一个新零件，但是还没收到。他们说零件这个月底就该到了，到时你就可以给我发传真了。

我给你写过很多信，但是我想你也没有收到。我曾托一个司机到卢萨卡去寄信，这样这些信就能更快地到你那里，但是可能他没有寄，所以我现在是从芒戈把信寄出去的。

## 第54页

所幸的是我回来了。孩子们和我的父母待在一起，但是我妈妈病得很重，我回来两周后她就过世了。这对我们大家来说是一段非常悲伤的日子。现在我不能离开孩子们，我无法回英国。我的妻子有了别人，她想和我离婚。但这需要时间。

郁子，我离开得如此匆忙。也许现在你已厌倦了等我，很快你就要回日本了。也许对你来说忘记我会更好。也许对你来说嫁给一个你自己国家的人会更好，而不是和一个尚无法娶你、过着迥异生活的人在一起。

可是我非常想念你。我无法离开赞比亚——但是你能来这里吗？我不知道对你来说是否可能过这种生活，但是当夜晚来临，我和孩子们坐在一起的时候，我希望你也和我们一起在这里。如果你仍然想见我，如果还有机会，请你设法来赞比亚。请来吧。我会在这里。

爱你的伯纳德

## 第55页

她看着信上方的日期：5 月 10 日。那天她已经离开英国了。她将近三个月没见过伯纳德了。

她找到一张纸开始写传真。

## 第 9 章　非洲的阳光，非洲的雨

### 第56页

当一个穿着校服的赞比亚小姑娘背着书包走进后院时，一只鸡匆匆从地面跑过。快五点了，但是九月的阳光仍然炙热，照得留在外面晾干的锅碗瓢盆闪闪发光。在院子的最里面有一棵大杧果树，长着宽阔的绿叶和很小的绿色果实。小姑娘向后门走去，并把书包扔在了门外的桌子上。房子只有一层，门在中间，两边各有一扇窗户。

“郁子，我回来了！”女孩儿叫道。

郁子走出来，来到热辣的阳光下。她看上去和几个月前打开伯纳德来信的那个脸色苍白、郁郁寡欢的女孩儿大不相同。她神色轻松，心情愉快。一个黑皮肤、大眼睛的小女孩儿紧紧抓着她另一只手。

“嗨，比阿特丽斯。在学校怎么样？”郁子问。

“很好。”比阿特丽斯用英语回答。然后比阿特丽斯和那个小女孩儿用她们自己的语言本巴语说了一会儿话。她又转向郁子。“查尔丽说今天你们去了市场。你买了一些西红柿和洋葱。”

### 第57页

郁子哈哈大笑。“是的，她帮我挑选的。都不错！”

“我爸爸回来了吗？”比阿特丽斯问。

“没有，他在照相馆呢。他很快就回来，然后咱们就吃晚饭。”郁子说。

“晚饭吃什么？”

"鸡肉和恩希玛，还有沙拉。"郁子回答。

"如果你想的话，我可以做恩希玛，"比阿特丽斯说，"对你来说太难了。我无法想象你们在日本不吃恩希玛是怎么生活的。"

郁子只是微笑。她不想告诉比阿特丽斯她觉得很难吃下难以消化的恩希玛。就是将面粉和水放在平底锅里，放在火上煮。但是孩子们爱吃，伯纳德也爱吃。

她到赞比亚差不多四个星期了。在某种程度上这四个星期是她人生中最快乐的时光。她惴惴不安地到达了那个小机场。她还会认得出他吗？如果他没在那儿接她，该怎么办？不过他来了，带着歪歪的笑容。他看上去没什么变化——除了不需要在热辣的太阳下穿红色夹克。他借了一辆朋友的车，他们从机场沿着低矮山丘和树木之间的狭窄道路一路行驶到家。到处都是干巴巴的，尘土飞扬。

### 第58页

"等到下个月雨季来临，"伯纳德说，"一切都会变绿。草会长得比房子还高。"郁子抬头看着蓝天，无法想象下雨的情景。这么空旷，她心想。这儿的天空看起来比她去过的任何地方都更广阔。

他们到达一座方正的房子前。那两个孩子羞涩地出来迎接他们。小查尔丽只是站着，吸吮着大拇指，目不转睛地盯着看。"她不大懂英语。"伯纳德说。

四周后，郁子和查尔丽彼此仍说不了太多话，但是小女孩儿似乎信任她。伯纳德和比阿特丽斯去学校时，她们在一起度过了很多时光。郁子发现做完所有的家务要花费很长时间——打扫、做饭、洗涮、熨烫。房子里有电灯，有一台冰箱和一台电视，但是没有洗衣机和电饭锅。

每天她和查尔丽走着去市场买菜。到那儿要走很远，回来要顶着烈日，提着很重的一袋子蔬菜。她看到非洲妇女背上背着自己的孩子，头上顶着买来的东西。看上去简单，但郁子试过，不行。回来时，她又热又累。接下来她坐在后门旁边的椅子上看查尔丽在花园里玩儿，感觉很愉快。

## 第59页

伯纳德回到家时，尽管经常已经是很晚了，但她总是很开心。他的照相生意已经开业了，所以教完课后他直接去那儿。生意不错，他晚上有很多工作要做。但是最终他总是回到家，他们会一起在屋外吃饭，沐浴着凉爽的晚风，听着黑暗中传来的虫鸣声，看着头顶上闪耀的繁星，直到孩子们困得迷迷糊糊去睡觉。

关于未来，他们还没有做任何决定。“等等看吧，”伯纳德说，“赞比亚不像英国或日本。我想让你留下，但你必须自己决定。”

接下来的一个星期，天越来越热。每天走着去市场更累了。小查尔丽一天中的大部分时间都躺在床上。每个人看起来都是又热又累。

## 第60页

“暑末是一段难熬的日子，”伯纳德说，“雨季来了会好一些。”

转天下午，雨来了。先是刮风，吹得院子里尘土飞扬。接着大大的雨滴落在干热的地面上。那气味很美妙，查尔丽笑着喊着，跑来跑去。

到晚上的时候雨还在下，外面的院子又湿又泥泞。比阿特丽斯和伯纳德回到家，衣服都湿透了。“雨季提前了，”伯纳德说，“可能不会持续太久，但是又凉快起来还是很不错的。”

第二天早上天气很好，但是下午又开始下起雨来。那天晚上郁子觉得小小的房子里似乎到处都是湿衣服和沾满泥的孩子。她意识到他们平日的生活有多少是在屋外面、在后门旁的大桌子上度过的。现在他们在屋内一言不发地吃着饭——伴着哗哗的雨声和隆隆的雷声，很难聊天。突然砰的一声巨响，所有的灯都灭了。“别担心，”伯纳德说，“只是断电了。比阿特丽斯，去拿蜡烛，然后去睡觉。”

暴风雨停了，伯纳德和郁子坐在烛光下相对无言。但这是一种让人不安的寂静，是两个人都在努力想该和对方说什么的寂静。

## 第61页

这时郁子开口了。“伯纳德，我很爱你，而且我也爱你的孩子。我想留在这里，但是我不知道我能不能行。”

“我明白，郁子。我想让你来这里，来看看这里是什么样子。但我知道这种生活对你来说不容易。”

“我想不是因为这个。自从雨季来临，生活会有一点儿艰难，但不是这个。可是，伯纳德，不论我到哪儿，我都想换个地方。我怎么了？为什么我就不能对自己已经拥有的感到满足？”

“你在寻找某种东西，郁子，但是你不知道那是什么。也许你最终会在日本找到它，在你自己的国家。”

“但是如果我走了，谁来照顾孩子们？”

“我应付得来，”伯纳德说，“不太容易，但是我能行。这不是问题所在。问题是我会失去你。我期望过我们能相守在一起，但是芒戈不是东京。尽管我爱伯明翰，我也不能一辈子住在那里。我想你也无法在芒戈生活下去，即使你已经努力尝试了。”

蜡烛燃尽了，他们的交谈还在继续。最终雨停了。“咱们去外面的长凳上坐吧。”伯纳德说。他们来到外面，坐到后门旁边的木凳上。云散了，非洲夜空中巨大的月亮又圆又亮。郁子伸出手，握住伯纳德的手。

## 第62页

“我想我必须走。我想最终我还是属于日本，但是我的一部分会一直在这里。我很高兴我来了。我很高兴我拥有我们在一起的这些回忆。也许我们不会再相见，但是在某种意义上我们会一直在一起，因为我们俩都会记得这些时光。”

* * *

那天早晨下过雨，但是此时阳光照耀在院子里的水洼上。郁子坐在房子外面的长凳上，旁边是她的蓝色旅行箱。比阿特丽斯和查尔丽在前门外，等着伯纳德的朋友开车过来。

伯纳德穿过后门走出来。他站在那里，看着她。“在那儿等一会儿。”他说着进屋去了。他拿着相机回来。这个日本姑娘回头看他，面无笑容。相机咔嗒一声，为今后的岁月记录下了这一瞬间。

# 第二部分　回家

## 第 10 章　飞往埃及的航班

## 第64页

埃及炙热的太阳在新成立的红海研究与旅游中心上空闪耀。阳光洒向那些低矮的白色建筑、毗邻的蓝色大海和绿色的空中的士停机场。这是 2050 年。微型空中的士看上去像天空中的昆虫一般飞来飞去，将乘客载到沿岸的海滩或马萨阿拉姆机场。

在研究中心，一位面容年轻、一头白发、穿着考究的女士正对着墙上的屏幕讲话。她像是阿拉伯人，但是她的英语没有口音。

“好，乔伊斯。嗯，如您所知，开幕式十一点开始，您的演讲将在总统讲话之后。那么，我们一个小时后见好吗？好。很好。那么再见。”屏幕黑了，那位女士转过身来。

在房间的另一边，两位男士从他们一直在研究的文件上抬起头。

## 第65页

“是乔伊斯·缪坦加吗？”两个人中个子较高的斯文问道。他一头金发，说话有瑞典口音。“她不相信提前到了，是吗，法蒂玛？”

法蒂玛一如既往地平静。“她打电话说他们刚刚到达马萨阿拉姆机场，所以她十分钟后就到这里。”

第二位男士看上去有些恼火。他是日本人，下巴尖尖的，头发搭在他黑色眼睛的上方，但是，像其他人一样，他讲英语。“还好她告诉我们了，”他生气地说道，“距开幕式只有一个小时了，她为什么就不早点儿打电话？”

法蒂玛哈哈大笑。“你永远捉摸不透乔伊斯，阿贵。生气没有用，她就是那样。不过我很高兴她同意演讲了。如果不是她做了很多事让大家了解我们在做的研究，那么我想这个中心就不会存在。她的确是一位优秀的传媒学者，是世界上最好的传媒学者之一，即使你不喜欢她这个人。”

“我很期待与她见面，”斯文说，“她是非洲人，是吗？”

“我想是的——虽然我不知道她是否真的在非洲生活过，”法蒂玛回答道，“她现在住在澳大利亚的悉尼。我想她多数时间都在那里生活。”

## 第66页

“她令人惊羡，”斯文说，“她的那些演讲太精彩了，你不知道她的报告融入了多少研究。她只有……多大？三十岁？”

“二十九岁，”法蒂玛说，“是的，你说得对，斯文。她才华横溢——她为海洋而生，为她的拍摄而生。不过很奇怪。她知道如何通过影片与人们交流，但当你和她见面时，其实很难跟她交谈。她似乎对人根本不感兴趣。”

那个日本人看上去仍然很生气。“我去年在琉球群岛工作的时候在那儿见过她。她潜入水中进行水下拍摄。我们当时很期待见到她。我们为她安排了一个聚会，但是她只待了十分钟。她跟我们在一起的整段时间里我们几乎没见到她。她独自就离开了——没有跟谁真正说过话。我记得她……美丽却自私，我觉得。冷冰冰的。”他一边回忆，一边摇头。

“好啦，我还是很高兴她来这里的——不管是不是冷冰冰的。”法蒂玛说道。

随着超声速飞机降落在马萨阿拉姆机场，乔伊斯·缪坦加关掉了戴在脖子上的视盘，然后伸展了一下她那棕色长腿。她很高兴要下飞机了，但是她并不期待接下来的几个小时。

## 第67页

由于她对法蒂玛及其团队正在做的工作很感兴趣，所以同意了在开幕式上演讲。但是尽管她毕生都在从事媒体工作，却从来不习惯与公众打交道。她不介意做演讲——面对数百名现场观众和数百万名电视机前的观众讲话。她知道她能自信地谈论自己的工作。她不喜欢的是演讲前后的应酬。要对她不认识的人彬彬有礼，跟那些只是因为她有名才想与她交谈的人客套。没关系，很快就会结束。转天她就将踏上返回悉尼的旅途。

她迅速下了飞机，直奔空中的士。她低头看着下面干燥的土地，心想着，回到非洲了。但是这里离家还很远。

全世界对海洋生命研究感兴趣的人都知道乔伊斯的名字。但是她出生在非洲中部，出生在一个没有海岸线的国家，那里的鱼要么是出现在超市冷柜里的，要么是市场上卖的那种鱼干。小时候，他们全家人还都住在一起的时候，她常常和父母一起去市场，而妈妈常常买些小鱼干来做饭。但她从来没见过活的、游动的鱼。她从未见过大海。

## 第68页

不过之后一切都变了。她妈妈搬到澳大利亚，开始了新生活。乔伊斯八岁时也来到了妈妈的身边。她站在悉尼的海滩上，注视着海浪拍打沙滩，非洲的生活已离她远去。

“我想下海。”她对妈妈说。妈妈只是大笑。不过乔伊斯的学校有一个游泳池，六个月后她在水中就和在地面上一样自信了。

她很快从泳池转移到了大海，十二岁时她完成了第一次潜水。一种新的人工鳃正在进行推广，它可以让潜水者从水中获得氧气，取代了笨重的水肺。乔伊斯感到非常兴奋，人工鳃能让她自由地探索水下世界，在那里，鱼不是冰冻的或者晒干的，而是活的，生活在它们自己的家园。

“就像飞一样，”她对妈妈说，“你感受不到重力，是完全自由的，就你自己。”

她开始用一台便宜的水下相机拍摄，把她看到的拍成视频。回到家，她再用电脑配字幕和音乐。她妈妈很担心她。“你才十五岁，”她说，“你正是应该开心地玩耍的时候，去参加聚会，结交朋友。”

但是乔伊斯不喜欢聚会，而且似乎也不需要朋友。到她十八岁准备开始在悉尼大学攻读传媒与海洋学专业时，她已经声名远扬。

她在网上工作，与全世界的海洋科学家建立联系。她已经找到了让自己生活充实而且得心应手的事情。她想这就是她想要的一切。

## 第 11 章　独自游泳

### 第70页

这个巨大的中央大厅里的观众如同身处大海深处，游弋在蓝色的海水中。不论他们看哪里——墙壁、地板、天花板——看上去都是水。乔伊斯的声音柔和却清晰，压过了音乐声。“而这就是为什么我相信这个项目只是一个开始。我们必须明白，海中的植物和鱼类是与我们共同生存，而不是为我们而生。我们必须为确保永不失去这份富饶和美丽而努力。”

随着乔伊斯的演讲结束，水消失了，墙壁和天花板又变成了白色。片刻安静之后，大厅内响起了掌声。在所有的演讲中，这将是所有人都会记住的一个。乔伊斯站在那里，等待着掌声停止。她笑了一下，接着又一脸严肃。

斯文低语道：“这太精彩了！太棒了！”

阿贵点了点头。“是的，”他拨开眼前的黑发说，“真是不错。”

### 第71页

乔伊斯确实是一位优秀的演讲者。阿贵注视着她从讲台上走下来，朝门口去了。

“快点儿，斯文。”阿贵说。

斯文和阿贵随着人群走向接待大厅，大厅是延伸出去建在海里的。有一面墙完全是玻璃的，在墙的另一面有小鱼在粉色和橘色的珊瑚间穿梭。乔伊斯站在一群人之中。她说话不多，而且看起来有些不高兴。斯文径直朝她走去。

“您好。我是来自瑞典的斯文·伯杰，”他说道，“我是红海中心这里的一个团队的成员。我可以单纯表达一下我对您的演讲和您的工作的喜爱吗？”

乔伊斯回头看他，不带一丝笑容。“谢谢。”她没有再说话。

“您会在这里多待些日子吗？”斯文继续说道，“我一直在努力研发一种新类型的水下电影。我想征求您的建议。”

“不行，”乔伊斯说，“不行，我想我没有时间。”斯文意识到她根本没在看他，而是看向他身后。沉默让人很尴尬，当他看到阿贵向他们走过来时，才感觉好些。

## 第72页

“您好，我是阿贵，”他冲乔伊斯礼貌地笑了笑说，“我相信我们以前见过。”

“是吗？”她问。

“去年您去琉球群岛的时候。”

“哦，”她回答道，“恐怕我不记得你了。不管怎样，不好意思，我现在得走了。”她转身朝门口走去。

阿贵和斯文面面相觑，抬了抬眉毛。“她或许是一位著名的传媒学者，但是她该学学懂礼貌了。”阿贵十分生气地说。

“冷静点儿，阿贵。她对谁都没兴趣，除了她自己，还有她的工作。那又怎样？得啦，咱们去喝一杯。我们应该开开心心的。”

乔伊斯强作镇定地离开了大厅。她知道她惹恼了那个日本人。但是她为什么应该记得她见过的每个人？她被介绍给全世界那么多的人。她从来无法记住人们的面孔，或者名字。除了鱼的名字。

她回到了紧邻中心的酒店，但是却放松不下来。四点了，还有整整一个晚上要度过。她想知道能不能现在就离开，但是如果还没有看看大海就走，会很遗憾。她换上泳装，穿上短裙，拿起人工鳃离开了房间。

## 第73页

正经过前台时，她听到有人喊她的名字。“乔伊斯！嗨……您要出去吗？”

是法蒂玛。乔伊斯不知道该说什么。她不想让法蒂玛跟她一起去。

“我想去散散步。”最后她说。

“那是您的人工鳃吗？您想游泳？”法蒂玛问。

“是的……也许就游一小会儿。这附近有什么地方可以游泳吗？”

“海岸附近就有一个项目人员使用的海滩。如果您愿意，我可以开迷你飞机送您过去。”

“我不想添麻烦。你一定很忙。”乔伊斯说。

“哦，不麻烦。我已经在紧挨着海滩的一家饭店给项目团队定了晚餐——只有我们三个人。我们希望您能加入。我们约在七点见面。现在顺路送您过去很快就能到，您游完泳就可以到饭店和我们一起进餐。”

乔伊斯似乎别无选择。“谢谢。”她说，然后跟着法蒂玛走出门。

## 第74页

小飞机悄声降落在一个空荡荡的海滩中央的沙地上。

法蒂玛转向乔伊斯。“您在这儿下——这是个好地方。这里离饭店走路只需要十分钟。现在是五点，所以在我们七点见面之前您有充足的时间。您喜欢一个人游？”

“是的，谢谢。”乔伊斯说着下了飞机，关上了身后的舱门。

乔伊斯在海滩上坐了许久，感觉肩膀被傍晚的太阳照得暖暖的。然后，随着夕阳西下，她拿着鳃走下海滩。她在水边停了下来，低头看着自己的双脚。因为离开酒店时很匆忙，她忘记带装脚蹼的包了。“我太愚蠢了。”她想。她水性非常好，但是如果脚上不穿脚蹼很难游很远。好吧，既然来了，就在附近游一会儿吧。她穿着轻便的网球鞋，但这里的海滩，水很清澈且多沙。她决定穿着鞋以防后面会遇到岩石。

齐腿深的海水最初是很温暖的，随着海越来越深，水也变得清凉。她能看见自己的白色网球鞋踩在黄澄澄的沙子上在水下泛着光。当水足够深时，她把面罩拉到脸上，打开人工鳃然后下潜。忽然间，她进入了一个新的世界。沙子在她的身下翩翩起舞，阳光穿过波浪照出各种各样的图案。接着沙子中开始出现岩石。色彩斑斓的小鱼在岩石间穿梭，它们离乔伊斯如此之近，她几乎能触碰到它们。

## 第75页

她出奇迅速地游到了暗礁，慢慢地向前，直到发现了一个有海底裂缝的地方。她游到了裂缝边缘。她估计身下距海底至少有三十米深，也许更深。但是比起忙碌的挤满人的接待大厅，这里可没那么可怕。她没有潜下去，而是沿着礁石边游，不时停下来仔细观察生活在那里的鱼和植物。

当她意识到渐渐看不清时，她游回了海面。她意识到自己下潜的时间比原想的长得多——太阳已经落到山那边了。至少她不必在饭店里待很长时间了。

由于没有脚蹼，她沿着礁石游回来花了很长时间。游到礁石的裂缝时，天几乎黑了。她朝陆地方向往回游，不时地露出头，以便查看游的方向对不对。现在太阳已经落山了，但是在她前面的山峦之后仍然有一抹余晖。她看不见身下的沙子，但她把脚伸下去时，脚触到了地面。离海岸还有最后几米，她站起来走了过去。晚风拂过她湿漉漉的身体，令她打了一个寒战。

### 第76页

此时海水刚没过她的膝盖。她又向前迈出一步，脚踢到了水下的什么东西，令她险些摔倒。接着她不停地尖叫起来。

## 第 12 章　石鱼

### 第77页

“我想她现在该到这儿了。”法蒂玛说。

法蒂玛、斯文和阿贵一起坐在饭店里，向水面望去。太阳几乎已经落山了，月亮正从海面升起，又圆又满。

“我想她已经回中心了，没告诉你而已。”阿贵说。

“但是她怎么回去啊？走路太远了。”法蒂玛说。她很担心。或许她不应该把乔伊斯独自留在那儿。“也许，我应该……”

这时他们听到远处黑漆漆的海滩那边传来一个声音。

“那是什么声音？”斯文问。他们又听到了一声，有人在尖叫。斯文和法蒂玛看了一下彼此。

“我们乘飞机过去，”法蒂玛说，“我们可能会需要飞机，而且飞机有灯。”

可是阿贵已经离开座位，奔了出去。他只能听到自己的呼吸声。他擅长奔跑，但大海在差不多 300 米远的地方，而且细软的沙子让人跑起来很费力，但是他知道每一秒钟都可能很重要。

## 第78页

在黑暗中听到她的哭喊声时，他差点儿要从乔伊斯的身边跑过去了。她坐在水里，半个身子露出水面，抱着一条腿。

“乔伊斯，你怎么了？”他问。

但她似乎没听到他说话。他俯下身去，努力扶她站起来，但她大声尖叫。他小心翼翼地把她抱起来，往岸上走了几步，然后把她放倒在沙地上。他在她旁边蹲下来。月光下，他看到她左脚的白鞋上有深色的血迹。他轻轻地摸了摸鞋底。有四个圆洞。他突然感到惊恐和气愤。

“你踩到石鱼了，”他说，“你那么了解大海，还穿着这样的鞋就出来了。你为什么不小心点儿？”

乔伊斯没有回答。她闭着眼睛，整个身体在颤抖。阿贵脱掉了她的鞋。她的脚已经开始肿起来。他看见石鱼背上锋利的毒刺深深扎进她脚里，留下了四处深色的印记。阿贵摸了摸她的腿。毒液已经向上转移。此时他更多是在自言自语，而不是对乔伊斯说话。

## 第79页

“四个洞。那是大量的毒液。她可能会失去这条腿——或者更糟。需要处置一下——要快。另外两个家伙到底在哪儿？”

一阵低沉的嗡嗡声从饭店那边传来。他抬起头看见在距地面约5米高的地方有盏灯正在靠近。飞机降落在几米开外的细软的沙滩上。法蒂玛向窗外大喊：“怎么了？出什么事了？”

“是乔伊斯。她踩到了石鱼，”阿贵说，“现在我们需要为她处置一下，然后把她送到医院。飞机上有医药箱吗？”

“有，在你的座位下，斯文——但是我不知道有没有治石鱼咬伤的。”

斯文拎着一个红箱子下了飞机。阿贵打开箱子。“很好。好，这里有一些有用的东西……如果我给她用这个，应该能对毒液有点儿作用。”他取出一个小塑料瓶，仔细查看了一番，然后打开瓶子的一端。他拿着瓶子对着乔伊斯的脚，按下一个小按钮。她一动不动。

“这样应该能阻断毒液。现在她得赶紧去医院。”

### 第80页

他抱起她，把她抱到飞机上，并小心地放到后面躺下。机舱前面还剩下一块地方。“你想跟我们一起去吗，阿贵？”法蒂玛问。

### 第81页

“不了，”阿贵说，“你们俩去。我需要走一走，喝一杯。她跟你们在一起会没事的。”

当那架小型飞机消失在夜空中时，阿贵穿过月色笼罩的沙滩走回饭店。“她为什么不小心点儿？”他又一次问自己。但是与其说他在生气，倒不如说他是难过。

## 第 13 章　白鞋

### 第82页

乔伊斯不知道自己在哪儿。由于石鱼的毒液和药物的作用，她脑子很混乱，感觉好像回到了水下，但这水很温暖。太温暖了……事实上，几乎是在灼烧她……或者也许是她在太阳底下待的时间太长了。在非洲你必须得当心炎热季节的太阳。她需要喝点儿什么——她口渴极了。

“妈妈！”她喊道，“爸爸！”

他们不会离得很远。他们为什么安顿她睡觉？乔伊斯决定从床上起来。她向下看……看到自己正穿着最好看的裙子，那件她六岁生日时得到的裙子，还有她白色的新鞋。但是她的鞋出了问题……她记不起是什么了。她对鞋子做了什么，所以她爸爸非常生气。她的脚疼，脚和腿。或许是那双白鞋弄疼了她。

“爸爸。”她听见自己在哭喊。

她挣扎着要起来，但是当她挪动腿时，疼得停了下来。她知道出事了。她躺在医院的病床上，白色的床单映衬着她的肌肤，在赞比亚那座小房子里，最后一天的情景又浮现了。

## 第83页

她穿着她崭新的白鞋出去玩儿。那时是雨季，道路泥泞。她一直在跟朋友们玩儿，弄得满鞋都是红色的泥。她在路边的一个小水塘里使劲儿洗，但鞋子看起来更脏了。

乔伊斯到家时，她爸爸冲她喊起来："你的新鞋！你为什么不小心点儿？"然后她妈妈进来开始冲她爸爸大喊。他们没有注意到小女孩儿去了自己的卧室。他们没有听见她是一个人哭着睡着的。

早上她爸爸去上班了，而妈妈已经收拾好了一个行李箱。她们两个人坐着公共汽车在泥泞的公路上颠簸了一整天，回到了芒戈，回到她外公家。她再也没见过她的爸爸。

乔伊斯睁开双眼，对俯身过来的医生说："你生气吗？因为我的鞋？"

"没有人生气。"医生说。乔伊斯愣了一会儿。"你是谁？你不是我爸爸。"她说。

"我是医生。你踩到了一条石鱼。你会没事的。"他看了一下她床边的电脑屏幕。"你需要休息。我给你开点儿药助眠。睡醒后你会感觉好些的，然后就可以见你的朋友了，好吗？”

## 第84页

“不……我谁也不想见。”乔伊斯说。她仍然感到困惑，感到在某种程度上自己表现得很差劲儿。她又睡着了，睡得并不安稳，敷着药的伤口仍然在疼。

她再次醒来时是独自一人。阳光透过窗户照进她那不大的私人病房。她的银色视屏上的时间显示为9点钟。她的腿不太疼了，但头疼，而且很渴。

门开了，一位女士端着早点走进来。乔伊斯并不饿，但喝了橙汁。阳光在病房的墙上移动着。她睡了一小会儿。她醒来时，床边的电脑屏幕上有一条信息。

“乔伊斯，我真的希望你没事儿。有什么我们可以帮你的吗？随时给我打电话，法蒂玛。”

但是她不想见法蒂玛。

一位护士进来查看，但乔伊斯闭着眼，于是她就离开了。混乱的记忆时隐时现。观众的掌声……一个男人愤怒的脸……有人抱着她。

## 第85页

她接下来知道的就是外面走廊上急促的脚步声。脚步声停了一会儿，接着门开了。乔伊斯仍然没睁眼。

“乔伊斯？”

这是她熟悉的声音，一个男人的声音。她突然记起水中的疼痛，记起有人怎么救起她……她记得这个声音，温柔但有些生气。

“是的……我本该小心点儿的。”她说。

她睁开了眼睛，看见了阿贵的脸。

## 第 14 章　探望

### 第86页

阿贵站在床边，低头看着躺在病床上的她，棕色的脸庞上一双黑眼睛显得很大，她的手静静地放在白床单上。突然间，她在他眼里看上去年龄很小，不再是那个惹恼他的强势女人，而是一个受了惊吓、几乎死在她热爱的大海里的女孩儿。

“对不起，我那样说话，”他说，“我以为你要死了。我很害怕。”

乔伊斯闭上眼睛。阿贵看到两行泪水顺着她的脸颊流下来。他下意识地伸出手，握住了乔伊斯的手。

“乔伊斯，你没事的。你会好起来的。”

“对不起。我不知道怎么了。我梦到……”她的声音很轻。

“我想是他们给你用药了。止疼的。”

“用了。”她说。

“那很可能是药物作用，但现在你应该没事了。你想让我叫什么人来吗？”

“不，谁也别叫。”乔伊斯闭上了眼睛。

“你累了吗？你想让我离开吗？”阿贵问。

### 第87页

她静默了一会儿，然后摇了摇头。“不，”她轻声说道，“在这儿待一会儿。”

阿贵握着她的手在床边坐了很长时间。他不确定她是醒着还是睡着了。这时她依然闭着眼，轻声说道：“阿贵……发生了什么事？”

“是一条石鱼。”他说。

他感觉到她的手握得更紧了。然后她睁开眼睛看着他。“我可能已经死了，是吗？如果你不在那儿的话。”

“有可能会。”他记起把她从黑漆漆的水中抱出来时她的身体因疼痛和寒冷而发抖的感觉。

她沉默了一会儿。她小心地动了动被子下的腿。

“还疼吗？”他问。

“疼，但比之前好多了。你认为我还得在这儿待多长时间？”

“不长。我想一周之后你就又能游泳了。”他尽量高兴地说。

她咬了咬嘴唇，突然看上去很疲倦。

“我得走了。”阿贵说。她点了点头，于是他放开了她的手。他不想离开她。

“如果你愿意的话，我今天晚上还来。”他提议。

## 第88页

她笑着说：“好的，我愿意。”

阿贵离开了病房，乔伊斯又独自躺在那儿。她想起她的梦。对赞比亚那天的记忆一直深藏在她的心底，要疼痛和药物才能唤起。现在她躺着思考着一切，思考着在那里曾是她生命的一部分的人，还有他们对她的意义。

阿贵从医院出来，热浪扑面。他回到研究大楼，在自己的电脑前坐了几分钟。但是他无法工作。他把乔伊斯的名字输入电脑，然后调出她演讲的录像。他回放了最后几分钟的镜头，灯光亮起，乔伊斯的脸部占据整个屏幕。他看着她深色的面庞、修长的脖子、高高的颧骨，以及演讲结束时那腼腆、歪歪的笑容。然后，没来由地，他把录像拷贝到了脖子上挂着的视盘里。

他站起来，在房间里不安地踱来踱去。就在那时，他脖子上的视盘发出嘟嘟声。来电话了。一位头发花白的日本老太太正站在花园里，她用日语跟他讲话。“阿贵，你看上去很不错。”她说。

### 第89页

“外婆！”

“但是你的头发该剪剪了！你就像你外公一样，从没有时间理发。头发挡眼了。”

阿贵笑出声来。他和外婆总是很亲近。阿贵是她孙辈中的老大，而且是唯一的男孩儿。

“我一直很忙！我们刚刚举行了中心开幕典礼。”他解释道。

“你知道你多长时间没来看我了吗？我想你该回来了。这个周末休假吧，你工作太辛苦了！周六见。”当她说完时，他的视盘又变黑了。

## 第 15 章　夜潜

### 第90页

那天晚上，乔伊斯坐在医院病房的窗边。她的左脚裹了一层薄薄的塑料膜。她向外眺望着落日余晖下的大海。仅仅 24 小时前她还在那片海域游泳，感觉在水里很安全自在。她想起水中潜藏的危险，不寒而栗。

她听到走廊上传来急促的脚步声，那几乎是在跑，紧接着门开了。她知道是谁，她笑着转过身。“阿贵！”她说。

“你感觉怎么样？”他问道。

“哦，没事。事实上，很好。”

“你又看医生了吗？”

“看了，”乔伊斯回答道，“他说我没事了。他说如果我愿意，今晚就可以出院了。我走路没问题了。虽然有点儿慢，但是脚完全不疼了。真让人难以相信，对吗？仅仅 24 个小时。医生说这是因为你处理及时。”

“哦，”阿贵说，“太棒了。”但是他似乎不相信。他停顿了一会儿。“那么你现在要去哪儿？”

## 第91页

“我想回家。”乔伊斯说。

“回悉尼？”阿贵问。

乔伊斯想起她在悉尼的那间小公寓，那是她旅途之间停顿的地方。但那是她的家吗？

“是的，我想是这样。”她轻声地说。

“你在那儿有家人吗？”阿贵问。

“没有……嗯，我妈妈过去住在那儿，但她现在住在美国。”

阿贵停顿了一下，然后语速变得很快。“你为什么不多待一两天呢？我可以给你看看我们在做的一些工作。”

乔伊斯抬眼看着他，犹豫不决。“我……我不确定。你不忙吗？”

“不忙。我有几天假。我们可以去游泳。你可以和我待在一起。”

“不！”乔伊斯说，她看到阿贵的眼睛睁大了。“对不起，我的意思是……我不想下海。”

她不知道该如何向他解释，一想到大海，想到那黑漆漆的海水，她就充满了恐惧。她感觉自己好像永远都不想再回到那儿了。

阿贵看着她。“医生说没说你可不可以游泳？”

## 第92页

“什么？”她慢吞吞地说。

“对，我们去潜水。就现在。你必须得回到大海——你必须得面对这种恐惧。”

乔伊斯向窗外望去。太阳几乎已经落山了，西边只有几抹红色。“我没说我害怕。”

他看着她。“你用不着说，我能看出来。我有过同样的经历——有一次我的鳃出了故障。唯一要做的就是直面它，但不是你独自面对，我们要一起来面对。”

“但是天黑了……”乔伊斯开口说。

“那么我们就来一次夜潜，”阿贵一跃而起，说道，“快点儿。你的鳃在这儿。我们需要的其他东西我都有。我们出去时告诉医生一声。”

乔伊斯发现自己正走出门去。

半小时后，他们坐上了一架迷你飞机。阿贵微笑着转过身来对她说：“我好长时间没有在夜里潜水了。我想你已经夜潜过好多次了吧？”

“对……但时间不长。”

“我们坐船到暗礁那里，这样我们就能直接到深水区。”他说。

他们在饭店的后面降落，五分钟后他们坐上了一艘小船。小船在平静的水面上静静地航行。月亮出来了，几乎是满月，月光在海面上照出一条白色的小路。在他们的前方，一条狭窄的白色区域表明暗礁的岩石露出了水面。然后他们穿过前一天她游到的那个暗礁裂缝。阿贵停下船。他递给她一个头灯，自己也戴上了一个。他们穿上脚蹼，戴上人工鳃。

## 第93页

“准备好了吗?”他问，然后他从船的一侧下了水。小船轻轻摇晃了一会儿，又恢复了静止。乔伊斯一只手扶在船舷上。水冷冰冰、黑漆漆的，她想着下面的水有多深。

“我不能下去。”她说。

阿贵从水里看着她。“乔伊斯，你必须下来。你能行。”

乔伊斯站起来。她犹豫了几秒钟，接着，她突然跳入水中不见了。

阿贵一时间很害怕。这时他看见水中有一盏灯向他移动过来。她的头露出来了，湿漉漉、亮晃晃的。

“太美了!”她说，“过来，阿贵。”她抓起他的手。

他们一起慢慢地游着，他白皙的身体挨着她黝黑的身体。珊瑚闪耀着红色和紫色的光芒，与白天的颜色很不一样。美丽的鱼儿受到乔伊斯和阿贵的灯光的吸引从礁石中的巢穴里游出来。乔伊斯不时地指这儿指那儿，阿贵的眼睛就会顺着她手指的方向看到一些很特别的鱼或者植物。

## 第95页

他们一起游到水面。阿贵摘掉自己的头灯，然后探过身子去摘乔伊斯的。满月映照在他们身上。远处饭店的灯光依稀可见，但在这儿只有他们俩。

“冷吗?”他问她。她摇摇头。

“我感觉很美妙，”她微笑着说，“谢谢你，阿贵。”

他向她伸出一只手把她拉向自己。她很轻松地就靠了过来，因为她的身体在水中是失重的。然后他亲吻了她，她尝到股海水的味道。

* * *

不到一个小时后，两人到了饭店。他们坐在外面，眺望着月光下黑漆漆的海水，等着上菜。

“你经常回日本吗？”乔伊斯问阿贵。

“我已经有一段时间没回去了，但我这周六要回去——去看望我外婆。”

第96页

“她多大年纪了？”乔伊斯问。

“哦……有 70 岁了，不太老。”

“你跟她很亲吗？”

“是的……我是她唯一的外孙。她总想让我去学习和旅行。我想她的生活并不精彩——上中学，上大学，在公司工作。她一结婚就不工作了，生下我妈妈。之后，再也没有重返职场。她和我外公过着平静的生活。她英语说得很棒，我小时候她常常让我跟她一起练。我不知道她怎么把英语学得那么好。”

“那么你外公呢？他还健在吗？”乔伊斯问。

阿贵笑了。“健在，我应该是长得很像他，但我看不出来。不过大家都这么说。”

“肯定很幸福。大家都在一起：父母、祖父母、孩子。我想，我就想要这样。”乔伊斯突然看上去很孤独。

阿贵伸出手，握住了她的手。“乔伊斯，你有没有考虑留在这儿？你必须回悉尼吗？难道你不能在这儿多待一段时间吗？”

“我住在哪儿呢？”她问。

“跟我住一起。”他说。

她摇摇头。“阿贵，”她说，“我……我愿意，但我认为我不行。”

她停了下来，不知如何表达。

## 第97页

“我知道。一切都发生得这么突然，但——”阿贵开口说。

“不，不是那样，是我真的不习惯跟别人在一起。我想我不擅长这个。我妈妈不擅长，我外婆也不擅长。她们俩都出走了。我妈妈离开我爸爸时把我带到了外公家。然后，她离开了赞比亚，在澳大利亚找到了一份工作。她把我留给了我外公。”

“你很不开心吧?”阿贵想到一个小姑娘被独自留下就问道。

“不……当时不是。刚开始我很想念我父母，但后来我跟外公在一起很快乐。”

她跟他讲述了自己那些年的生活。她和朋友一起从小学一路走回家里的小房子，脚上的红色尘土暖暖的。她跟外公一起坐在后屋外写作业。没有人看见的时候，她就爬上杧果树吃甜甜的黄色水果。

接着，她收到了妈妈的信。妈妈在澳大利亚找到了一份很好的工作，也已经为乔伊斯联系了一所学校。她想让她回到身边。

“我哭啊哭啊。我不想去澳大利亚，我甚至不知道那是哪儿。但是我去了，然后我就发现了大海。大海看上去很安全，它永远都在那儿。”

## 第98页

“是啊。”阿贵说。他开始理解。“但是你外公呢?”他问。

“我真的很想他。我们过去有时通信，一年左右一次，纸的书信。他不喜欢其他形式的信息。他不愿意用视盘。我还去看过他一两次，每次只有几天。但是最近几年我一直很忙……后来我从姨妈——我妈妈的妹妹那儿收到消息。就在我来这儿之前，他去世了，享年 80 岁。”

“对不起。”阿贵说。

“我甚至不知道他生病了，”乔伊斯继续说道，“但是我今天在医院时在想他。我想我要回去，只是再去看看那个地方。”

阿贵沉默了许久。乔伊斯开始感到紧张，她以前从来没有跟人谈论过这么多关于她自己的事。她从未遇见过她想要把自己的故事讲给对方听的人。

“乔伊斯，你肯定累了。来吧，我送你回酒店。”阿贵主动提议。

不久之后他们走进酒店。阿贵等乔伊斯去拿房间钥匙。服务员把钥匙给她，然后又递给了她别的什么东西。乔伊斯低头看了一会儿，然后向阿贵走去。

## 第99页

“看。”她把东西交给他。那是一个纸信封，看上去又旧又脏，好像有许多人摸过。乔伊斯的悉尼住址已经被勾掉，这封信是被改寄到埃及的酒店的。信封的背面有一个名字和地址：伯纳德·奇卢巴，赞比亚北部省芒戈市卡萨马路 42 号。

“伯纳德·奇卢巴？”

“我外公。这封信花了三周的时间到我手里。肯定是在他弥留之际写的。”

他把信交还给她。她慢慢地打开信封，一把钥匙从里面掉出来，掉到地上。阿贵弯腰捡起它，是一把旧的金属钥匙。他拿着钥匙，而乔伊斯看起信来——手写的一页纸。然后她把这封信交给他。

亲爱的乔伊斯：

我想给你写信是因为我知道我们该说再见了。我已经活得够久了。我希望你什么时候能回到芒戈来，我的房子在等你。这是钥匙。你会在你过去住的卧室里找到一些箱子，是留给你的。或许你在那儿会找到一些要看的东西。

## 第100页

我希望这个房子会成为一个你歇脚的地方，或者当你有了家庭后能把家人带过来。你妈妈从未找到一个能够让她快乐的地方，你外婆也是。我很抱歉没能给她们这样一个地方，但是我希望，在这个小小的世界上，你能找到一个自己停留的地方。

爱你的外公

“我必须走了，”乔伊斯说，“我从这里乘飞机，明天就能到那儿了。我现在就去问问机票的情况。我可以直飞卢萨卡，然后换乘……”

阿贵摇摇头。“乔伊斯，今晚你不能再做任何事了。你需要睡觉。潜水之后发生了这么多事，今晚我本不该把你带去那儿的。”

她看着他。“我很高兴你带我去了。”

“我会帮你订好航班，”他说，“反正我也需要买去日本的机票。明天早晨我来这儿接你，我们可以一起吃早点。”

# 第 16 章　一本白色日记本

## 第101页

结果，三天后他们才订票。三天里，他们在海边游泳，打发漫长而慵懒的时光，然后回到阿贵的公寓冲掉身上的盐和沙子。

直到第三天早晨，阿贵醒来伸了个懒腰，然后说："乔伊斯，今天星期几？"

乔伊斯睁开眼睛。"有什么关系吗？"

但是阿贵已然在房间里飞奔起来。"今天是星期五。外婆，我答应她明天就到的。我的视盘在哪儿？我得去买票。乔伊斯，你想跟我一起去吗？"

她大笑。"不。记住——我要去芒戈。"

他停下，走过来紧挨着她坐在床上。"不过你会回来吧？你不会就消失了吧？我们还没有谈过。"

"我们已经聊了三天了。"她说。

"是，但是还没说我们下一步怎么办。"

"别担心，"乔伊斯说，"就订机票吧。"

那天晚上，阿贵跨越半个地球到达了他旅程的最后一站。他沿着外婆住的那条静谧的马路走着。房子只有两层高，但有六十多年的历史，在日本是非常古老了。他向门口走去，门开了。他听到外婆的声音在喊："阿贵，快进来。我在客厅。"她坐在她那把低矮的椅子上，花白的头发环抱着白皙的面庞，看上去比她实际年龄要小。

## 第102页

"你总算来了。"他走进房间时她说。

阿贵抬起手拨开眼前的头发。

"哦，你还是老样子。你的头发还是太长，就像你外公一样。"她继续说。

"外公在哪儿？"阿贵问。

"出去了。他很快就回来。对了，给我讲讲你都在做什么。你看上去很好，很轻松。”

“是的。”他不知道有多少事要讲给外婆听。不知道她会听懂多少。她可能梦想着给她唯一的外孙娶一个漂亮的日本媳妇。

“那么你们的研究中心现在开始了吗？开幕式顺利吗？”

“非常顺利。我们邀请到了总统出席，而且请到一位赞比亚研究员做了一场精彩的开幕演讲。她是一位传媒学者，拍水下电影的。”

## 第103页

他的外婆挺了挺身子坐直了一点儿。“赞比亚人。很有意思，”她说，“我想看看。”

“好，如果您感兴趣，我可以给您看看那个演讲，我拷到我的视盘上了。”

他打开视盘，找到那段录像，然后把视盘递给外婆。但是她似乎对海洋生命并不感兴趣。她快进到最后一部分，乔伊斯演讲的特写出现了。她暂停了录像，更仔细地看着。阿贵从她的肩头看过去，录像里乔伊斯看过来，带着羞涩的、歪歪的笑容，这种笑容他在过去的几天里经常见到。

“她是一个可爱的姑娘，”他的外婆说道，“她叫什么名字？”

“乔伊斯，乔伊斯·缪坦加。”

他外婆看着他。“奇怪，一个赞比亚女性研究海洋生命。赞比亚不靠海。”

他惊讶地看着她。他不知道外婆还听说过赞比亚。“她在悉尼长大。”他回答。

“哦，那你认识她？”外婆问。

他不知道该说什么，但是他想给外婆讲讲这个新进入他生活里的人。

## 第104页

“是的，”他说，“我认识她。”然后他给她讲了过去五天里发生的故事。

“所以您知道，”他最后说，“她回这个村庄去了，回到了芒戈。回到她和她外公一起生活过的那个房子。然后她会给我打电话，我们会见面。我不知道在哪儿见。这没关系，但是我确信我们会见面的。”

在讲故事的过程中，阿贵的外婆变得非常安静。“我对不起伯纳德。”阿贵讲完时她低声说。

阿贵困惑地看着她。伯纳德是谁？然后他想起那是乔伊斯给他看的那个信封上的名字，是乔伊斯外公的名字。可是他肯定没对外婆提过那个吧？

过了一会儿，他外婆站起身，走向壁橱。她伸手进去，摸到后面，拿出了一个白色的小本子。阿贵注意到她的手在颤抖。

“阿贵，我想把这个给你，”她说，“这是很多年前，嫁给你外公之前，我写了好几个月的一本日记，我从没给任何人看过。我想让你看看，或许乔伊斯也想看看。我现在感觉有点儿累，我想我该休息了。”

## 第105页

阿贵接过日记本。在封皮上有一个名字：金泽郁子。

“金泽？”他说。

“那是我结婚前的名字。”她闭上了眼睛。

他小心地把日记本放入包内，然后站起身。他的外婆又开口说话，可她的眼睛依然闭着。“下次你来的时候，把乔伊斯·奇卢巴带来吧。”

“她是乔伊斯·缪坦加，外婆。”

“没关系，来自芒戈的乔伊斯。”

## 第 17 章　一箱照片

### 第106页

乔伊斯让出租车停在芒戈的卡萨马路的拐角处，然后下了车。她想用双脚走完最后的旅程。她几乎认不出村中心了。新的高楼大厦矗立在那里，那儿的旧市场已经不复存在，老学校变成了开放教育中心。不过沿途的景物变化不大。房子看上去比她记忆中的小，街道也更窄，但她那时只是个八岁的小女孩儿。

此时雨季已经结束，路面很干燥。乔伊斯向 42 号走去。窗帘紧闭，她从包中掏出那把金属钥匙打开了前门。

她走进那间又热又暗的客厅。外公的卧室在最左侧，而厨房和她的房间在后面。她打开外公的房门，床收拾得整整齐齐，窗帘拉着。屋里非常整洁，太整洁了。

### 第107页

她迅速关上门，来到她曾经的房间，之前也是她妈妈和姨妈小时候睡过的房间。房间里有两张很窄的床。乔伊斯坐在自己的那张床上。她回想起了那些夜晚，她躺在床上，而外公在客厅看着旧电视或听音乐。没有争吵，没有大声嚷嚷，只有她和外公。她意识到自己在这里感受到了家的感觉。这是唯一的地方吗？她想起阳光透过阿贵公寓的窗户。不，现在肯定还有别的地方、别的人。但是在这里依然感觉很好。

她坐在房间里环视四周。一个角落里堆放着箱子，箱子上面盖着落满灰尘的塑料布。她扯掉塑料布，看着那些箱子。有一些箱子标注了日期。日期可以早到六十多年以前。乔伊斯尽可能多地搬起箱子，把它们搬到外面，然后坐在房后的旧木凳上。

那是一条长木凳——小的时候她时常在炎热的下午躺在那上面睡觉。即便在那时候，长凳已经很破旧了。乔伊斯还记得长凳坏了的时候外公是如何修理的。现在，已经过去二十年了，它又坏了。但是是可以修理的，乔伊斯想。杧果树还在庭院的尽头，准备好了让小孩子们去攀爬。

### 第108页

她把落满灰尘的箱子放在了身旁的座位上，然后在牛仔裤上擦了擦手。她打开一个箱子，箱子上标注着 2010 年。箱子里面装满了照片：四十年前芒戈的新郎和新娘的彩照。他们现在应该已到中年了。他们中很少有人会仍然住在这个小镇上——就像她的家人一样，而是生活在非洲各地，甚至世界各地。

她看了看其他箱子上的日期：2012 年、2007 年、2002 年。有一个箱子没有标注日期，但上面写着“英国”。她小心地打开箱子，然后取出一堆大幅的黑白照片：一个姑娘在教堂注视着一块墓碑，一个留着黑色直发、下巴尖尖、皮肤白皙的姑娘，一个日本姑娘。接着是一个非洲男子的照片，他坐在一栋很大的老房子前面的一堵墙上。墙上有一个牌子——奥克路。她仔细地看那个男人。他让她想起了谁？

这时一张彩色的小照片正面朝下掉在了地上，照片背面写着字。她捡起来看上面的字：伯明翰张伯伦广场，2000 年 4 月。五十年前了。她把照片翻了过来，那个非洲男子和那个日本姑娘一起站在大广场上。乔伊斯凑近了看，她确定了。那是她的外公，看上去年轻且身材修长，不是她记忆中的那个头发灰白、体型健壮、满脸皱纹的外公。他一只手拿着相机，身上穿着一件红夹克。他搂着那个一头黑发的年轻日本姑娘。他们的脸上洋溢着幸福的光芒。

## 第109页

乔伊斯回头向箱子里看了看，在箱子底部还有一张黑白照片。乔伊斯把它拿起来。照片上是那个日本姑娘，但这一次她穿着夏装坐在房子外面的一条长凳上。那个姑娘看上去年纪更大些了吗？很难说。还是尖下巴和黑眼睛，但这张照片里她的眼中没有笑意。有一刻乔伊斯感到这双眼睛仿佛在看她。那个姑娘坐在一个看上去几乎崭新的木凳上，在她面前的地上有一个旅行箱。

乔伊斯转身看她坐的那张长凳，与照片里那个姑娘坐的凳子一模一样。凳子后面是外公房子的窗户。这么说那个日本姑娘来过这里，而她的外公去过英国。他从未跟她讲过他去过英国，也没有提过任何来自日本的客人。她想知道那个姑娘是谁，他们是如何相遇，又为何分开的。她想知道这个姑娘是否知道故事的全部。

## 第110页

她在阳光下坐了一会儿，然后她拿起她的视盘，按下一个按钮。她说话的声音很轻柔。“嗨，我在芒戈，我就在外公房子的外面。”在屏幕上她看到了一个男人的脸，面庞年轻，黑色的头发垂落到眼前，还有着尖尖的下巴。他的眼睛从世界的另一边向屏幕外看过来。她继续说话。“我有东西要给你看……但不是在视盘上。我想让你到这里来，阿贵。”

“乔伊斯，我也有东西让你看，”他说道，“你一定要看的东西。我已经在飞机上了，我来了。”

乔伊斯把照片放回箱子里，她想稍后再看其余的照片。她坐下来看看周围，这个房子里还有很多活儿要干。这可真是个疯狂的安家之所，距大海有 1000 千米。但在这里，也许有些故事过早地画上了句号，有些故事又可能会开始。